30

SEASONS AT

ST JAMES' PARK

1974-75 TO 2003-04

David Powter

CONTENTS

British Library Cataloguing in Publication Data
A catalogue record for this book is available from the British Library

ISBN 1-86223-094-3

Printed by The Cromwell Press

NEWCASTLE UNITED – 30 SEASONS 1974-1975 TO 2003-2004

INTRODUCTION

Founded in 1882, Newcastle United F.C. is one of England's most famous clubs. It's supporters are renowned for being among the most passionate in the land. All-told the club has won 11 major trophies (four League titles and seven cups) and during the 30 years up to the summer of 2004 the Magpies went close to adding to their trophy haul on several occasions. They were twice Premiership runners-up, on three occasions reached Wembley Cup Finals and, as recently as 2003-04, reached the last four of the UEFA Cup.

Newcastle's most recent major trophy success came in 1969 when they lifted the European Inter-Cities Fairs Cup. Under the stewardship of Joe Harvey, they enjoyed three consecutive European campaigns. The Magpies also won the 1972-73 Anglo-Italian Cup and, one year later, lifted the Texaco Cup.

Their League form in 1973-74 was mixed and they only finished two points above the relegation line, in 15th place. In contrast, Harvey's side reached the F.A. Cup Final where they met Bill Shankly's Liverpool. Unfortunately, Newcastle badly froze on the day and were comfortably beaten 3-0.

1974-1975 SEASON

There was a notable departure from St James' Park during the 1974 close season when long-standing captain Bobby Moncur joined local rivals Sunderland. The former Scotland skipper made 296 League appearances (and scored 3 goals) for the Magpies. He also performed courageously in many cup-ties, most notably during those two crucial Fairs Cup Final encounters (when he scored three vital goals).

The Magpies made a promising start to 1974-75, winning five of their first nine League fixtures to lie in sixth place. However, they gradually drifted into mid-division. Their slide became more dramatic towards the end of the campaign and, after only winning one of their final 11 games, they had to be content with 15th place. 21-goal Malcolm Macdonald was the leading scorer, while his strike partner John Tudor contributed 14 goals. Willie McFaul retired at the end of the campaign after making 290 League appearances between the posts for the Magpies.

Joe Harvey's side reached the quarter-final stage of the League Cup in 1974-75, knocking out Nottingham Forest, Queen's Park Rangers and Fulham. However, they were surprisingly defeated at Sealand Road by Fourth Division Chester City in a replay. Hopes of reaching another F.A. Cup Final evaporated in the mud at Third Division Walsall (in the fourth round).

The one crumb of cup joy in 1974-75 came in the Texaco Cup. The Magpies retained the trophy by defeating Southampton at the end of extra-time of the two-legged Final.

JOE HARVEY

Reign: 1962-1975
Honours: Inter-Cities Fairs Cup and Division Two Champions
Highest League finish: 7th in 1969-70
Best F.A. Cup Run: Final in 1973-74
Best League Cup Run: Quarter-final in 1974-75
Best European Run: Inter-Cities Fairs Cup Winners in 1968-69

1975-1976 SEASON

After the disappointment of 1974-75, the St James' Park faithful were a rather discontented bunch in the summer of 1975. Consequently Joe Harvey bowed to public opinion and relinquished his position as manager after 13 seasons at the helm. The former Newcastle skipper had turned an average Second Division side into trophy winners and a respected top-flight side. Harvey remained at the club almost up to his death (in 1989) working in the back-room and all-told worked for the club for nearly 37 years.

The new manager was Gordon Lee, who arrived after a contractual tug-of-war with his previous employers Blackburn Rovers.

The Magpies lost all four of their games in the early season Anglo-Scottish tournament; but in contrast, later in the campaign, embarked on two long runs in the major cup competitions.

Lee's side knocked out Southport, Bristol Rovers, QPR and Notts County en route to a two-legged League Cup semi-final with Tottenham Hotspur. The London side held a 1-0 advantage after the first match, but the Magpies really came to grips with their task at St James' Park. Roared on by the bulk of the 51,000 crowd, they earned a trip to Wembley with goals by Alan Gowling, Geoff Nulty and Glen Keeley. With Spurs scoring just once in reply, Newcastle triumphed 3-2, on aggregate, to book a place in the Final against Manchester City.

A Wembley full house enjoyed fine entertainment, but the black and white army faced the bitter disappointment of another Cup Final defeat. City won 2-1 with Gowling netting for the Magpies. City's winning goal was an acrobatic bicycle-kick by Newcastle-born Dennis Tueart. The remainder of the Newcastle team at Wembley on 24th February 1976 was: goalkeeper Mike Mahoney, Irving Nattrass, Alan Kennedy, Stewart Barrowclough, Pat Howard, Micky Burns, Tom Cassidy, Malcolm Macdonald, Tommy Craig and Keeley.

Hopes of F.A. Cup glory increased as QPR, Coventry City and Bolton Wanderers were side-stepped en route to the quarter-final stage. Sadly, Lee's injury-hit side subsided 4-2 to Derby County at the Baseball Ground.

Newcastle could not maintain any consistency in the 1975-76 League campaign and again finished in 15th place. Gowling netted 16 League goals (30 in all competitions), but for the fourth time in five seasons it was Macdonald who was the club's leading League goalscorer (with 19). However, very controversially, Lee sold him to Arsenal (for £333,333) in the close-season. Lee was not good at handling the stars and Supermac was then one of the biggest names around. Macdonald's scoring record for Newcastle United (following his transfer from Luton Town) was a wonderful 95 goals from 187 League games.

1976-1977 SEASON

Six months after selling after Malcolm Macdonald, Gordon Lee also left St James' Park. With the Magpies on the heels of the leaders, in fifth place, and 18 months of his contract outstanding, Lee accepted an offer to manage Everton. He decided that it would be in the best interests of his family to work closer to where his children were being schooled (in Lancashire). He was never forgiven for selling Supermac.

The players petitioned the board of directors to request that Lee's assistant Richard Dinnis be given the chance to manage the club. Initially Dinnis was appointed on a temporary basis, but after further unrest by some of the players, he was appointed team manager for the remainder of the season. An 11-game unbeaten run gave Newcastle an outside chance of taking the title, but they 'blew-up' badly losing four of their final five fixtures and had to settle for fifth place. Nevertheless, it was a fine achievement considering the mid-season unrest and earned them another chance to play in Europe. Micky Burns netted 14 times to be the club's top scorer, while the promising Paul Cannell contributed 12 goals, one more than Alan Gowling.

Newcastle United were defeated 7-2 by Manchester United, at Old Trafford, in the fourth round of the League Cup. While Manchester City halted their F.A. Cup run, at St James' Park, also in the fourth round.

GORDON LEE

Reign: 1975-1977

Honours: None

Highest League finish: 15th in 1975-76

Best F.A. Cup Run: Quarter-final in 1975-76

Best League Cup Run: Final in 1975-76

1977-1978 SEASON

With Richard Dinnis now the full-time manager, the Magpies started 1977-78 with a victory, but then lost a club record ten consecutive League games to lie bottom of the table. In addition to this, Second Division Millwall knocked them out of the League Cup at St James' Park. However, some comfort was gained in the UEFA Cup, where they defeated Bohemians 4-0, on aggregate in the first round.

In the second round they met Bastia and, despite losing the away leg 2-1, United were favourites to reach the third round. However, it was the French side (who went on to reach the Final) that most enjoyed the game at St James' Park, winning 3-1 (and 5-2 on aggregate). The writing was on the wall for Dinnis and, with exactly one third of the season gone, he was dismissed with Newcastle lying in 21st place – having accumulated just six points.

Bill McGarry was appointed as the new manager and, after three straight wins in December, Newcastle's prospects looked somewhat brighter. However, they were knocked out of the F.A. Cup by Third Division Wrexham (4-1 away in a fourth round replay) and won only once more in 23 League games. Consequently they were relegated in 21st place. Less than 8,000 turned up to watch the final home game, by which time the Magpies had been consigned to the Second Division after a gap of 13 seasons.

Tommy Burns was the top scorer, with 15, but no other player netted more than five times as United scored their goals at exactly one goal per game. During 1977-78, David Craig wore a Newcastle shirt for the 351st and last time in the League (8 goals), while Stewart Barrowclough (219 games – 21 goals) made his final League appearance before joining Birmingham City.

RICHARD DINNIS

Reign: 1977
Honours: None
Highest League finish: 5th in 1976-77
Best F.A. Cup Run: None
Best League Cup Run: Round 2 in 1977-78

1978-1979 SEASON

Bill McGarry quickly rebuilt the team, spending a lot of money on the likes of Peter Withe, John Connolly, Colin Suggett, Mark McGhee and Jim Pearson. Terry Hibbitt was also signed for his second spell at the club. McGarry's side halted a club record winless run in the League by beating Luton Town at the end of August. They were among the Second Division's top five at Christmas, then disaster struck and they lost seven out of eight games. They eventually had to be content with eighth place. Withe was the leading scorer (with 14), while Alan Shoulder netted 11 times. Irving Nattrass made his 238th and last League appearance (16 goals) for the Magpies during the campaign before joining Middlesbrough.

There was little joy on Tyneside in the cups in 1978-79. Third Division Watford knocked Newcastle out of the League Cup and Wolves got the better of them in a fourth round replay, at Molineux, in the F.A. Cup.

1979-1980 SEASON

The results matched the burning optimism for more than half of the 1979-80 campaign, and with 16 fixtures left, Bill McGarry's side sat proudly on the top of the Second Division. However, they won just once more and threw away their chance of promotion, finishing in ninth spot. 20-goal Alan Shoulder was the main marksman, while Peter Withe netted 11 times.

Newcastle failed to win a cup tie in 1979-80, exiting both competitions at St James' Park. They lost a penalty shoot-out to Sunderland in the League Cup and were beaten 2-0 by Third Division Chester City in the F.A. Cup.

1980-1981 SEASON

Newcastle made a dismal start to 1980-81 and Bill McGarry was sacked and replaced by Arthur Cox. The relatively unknown Chesterfield manager was a surprise choice. The Magpies were woeful up front all term, netting just 30 goals and only twice scoring as many as three times in a match (the second occasion being the last day win against Orient). Newcastle set a new club record of failing to score in 23 League games (16 of those games were at St James' Park). Bobby Shinton was the top scorer, with seven goals. Alan Shoulder and Mick Harford netted four goals apiece.

The defence was not exactly rock solid either, with the side losing 4-0 at both Bolton and Swansea, and being hammered 6-0 at Chelsea.

Thus, it remains somewhat of a mathematical freak that Newcastle United's final placing in the Second Division table was as high as 11th, even though they were just six points above the relegation line.

Former Tow Law forward (and future England international) Chris Waddle made his debut in the October fixture at home to Shrewsbury Town.

There was some cup joy in 1980-81, with Sheffield Wednesday and Luton Town being beaten in the F.A. Cup. However, that run came to an embarrassing end when Third Division Exeter City beat them 4-0 in a replay in Devon. Earlier in the campaign Fourth Division Bury tipped the Magpies out of the League Cup.

BILL McGARRY

Reign: 1977-1980
Honours: None
Highest League finish: 21st
Best F.A. Cup Run: Round 4 in 1977-78 and 1978-79
Best League Cup Run: Round 2 in 1978-79, 1979-80 and 1980-81

1981-1982 SEASON

The arrival of Imre Varadi gave the team more fire-power in 1981-82. Hopes of scrambling into the promotion frame remained good until they lost six games out of seven during the run in. Newcastle finished with two victories to be ninth. There were three ever-presents in 1981-82: goalkeeper Kevin Carr, the top scorer Varadi (with 18) and the second highest scorer Chris Waddle (with 7). Only 4,026 witnessed their defeat at Orient, in November, a post-war club record low gate to watch a

Newcastle League game.

Third Division Fulham beat the Magpies, home and away, in the League Cup, while Grimsby Town won 2-1 at St James' Park in the F.A. Cup fourth round.

1982-1983 SEASON

Arthur Cox pulled off a master-stroke during the summer of 1982, when he enticed 31-year-old Kevin Keegan to move to Tyneside from Southampton. Keegan (whose father and grandfather hailed from County Durham) scored on his debut at St James' Park in front of over 36,000 and went on to net 21 times to finish as the club's joint top scorer (with Imre Varadi). With Terry McDermott rejoining the club from Liverpool, hopes were high that some great times were around the corner.

Certainly 1982-83 was Newcastle United's best campaign for some while; but it took them time to hit a vein of consistency. The season's end came just too soon for Keegan & Co. They just missed out on promotion, by three points in fifth spot.

The Magpies crashed out at the first hurdle of the League Cup against Leeds United, while Brighton & Hove Albion spun them out of the F.A. Cup in a third round replay at St James' Park.

1983-1984 SEASON

The final piece in Arthur Cox's jigsaw was completed in the early part of 1983-84 when Peter Beardsley joined from Vancouver Whitecaps (for just £120,000). Kevin Keegan netted 27 times, Beardsley scored 20 goals and Chris Waddle contributed 18 as the Magpies rattled up 85 goals on their way to gaining promotion. Only two of their last 16 games ended in defeat, but Cox's side could not quite get on terms with the top two – Chelsea and Sheffield Wednesday – and finished nine points adrift in third place.

Terry McDermott and Waddle were ever-present in 1983-84, with Keegan missing just one game. John Anderson and Ken Wharton also featured in 41 games, while David McCreery was absent only twice. The mid-season arrival of the classy Glenn Roeder (from QPR) helped to strengthen the defence.

There was no cup run of any degree to distract Cox's squad in 1983-84. Third Division Oxford United knocked them out of the League Cup and Liverpool defeated them 4-0 at Anfield in the F.A. Cup.

Keegan (who scored 48 League goals in 78 League games for the Magpies) retired from playing after scoring in the final 1983-84 fixture against Brighton & Hove Albion, in front of another 36,000 plus St James' Park crowd. But a considerably bigger shock was Arthur Cox's resignation 12 days later. Cox left to take over as manager of Derby County (who had just been relegated to Division Three). And, apparently, he accepted a lower salary in order to make the move.

ARTHUR COX

Reign: 1980-1984
Honours: None
Highest League finish: 3rd in Division Two in 1983-84
Best F.A. Cup Run: Round 5 in 1980-81
Best League Cup Run: Round 2 in 1981-82, 1982-83 and 1983-84

1984-1985 SEASON

Arthur Cox's replacement was Ashington-born Jack Charlton, who had previously managed Middlesbrough and Sheffield Wednesday. After six seasons in the Second Division, Newcastle United's return to the top-flight began with three successive victories, which took them to the top of the First Division for the first time in 34 years. However, they quickly came down to earth, conceding 10 goals in three defeats before throwing away a 4-0 lead on QPR's artificial pitch in a 5-5 draw. They slipped into the bottom half in November and remained there for the remainder of 1984-85 without really being sucked into the relegation dog-fight. Nevertheless they only finished three points above relegated Norwich City, even though their position was a misleading 14th place.

During the latter part of the campaign, 17 year-old Paul Gascoigne was introduced from the bench on two occasions. 17-goal Paul Beardsley was the club's leading scorer, while Chris Waddle netted 13 times. The 1984-85 campaign was Waddle's last at St James' Park before his move to Spurs for a club record £590,000 fee. Waddle netted 46 times in 170 League games for the Magpies.

There was disappointment in the F.A. Cup at St James' Park, when Newcastle were beaten 3-1 in a third round replay by Nottingham Forest. They also exited the League Cup to Ipswich Town on the same ground in another third round replay.

JACK CHARLTON

Reign: 1984-1985
Honours: None
Highest League finish: 14th
Best F.A. Cup Run: Round 3 in 1984-85
Best League Cup Run: Round 3 in 1984-85

1985-1986 SEASON

Jack Charlton resigned at the start of 1985-86. The World Cup winning centre-half had been barracked by some fans in a friendly match with Sheffield United. In addition, he had a disagreement with his board. After ten years as the club coach, Willie McFaul stepped up to take the managerial reins. The former goalkeeper became the sixth man to hold the position in ten years.

Newcastle United were well placed in fourth spot after ten fixtures, but despite five straight wins in the new year, they gradually slipped to finish 11th. Peter Beardsley was again the leading scorer (with 19) and both he and Glenn Roeder were ever-present. Paul Gascoigne held down a regular place in the side and contributed nine goals and many more assists. Newcastle's worst defeat came near the end of the season, when they were hammered 8-1 by West Ham United. The Magpies were forced to field three men between the posts in this game. The injured Martin Thomas was replaced by Chris Hedworth. The substitute keeper also collected an injury and had to be replaced by Beardsley.

McFaul's side enjoyed little success in the cups. Oxford United knocked them out of the League Cup and Second Division Brighton & Hove Albion beat them 2-0 at St James' Park in the F.A. Cup third round.

1986-1987 SEASON

The Magpies made a dreadful start to 1986-87, picking up only two points from the first six games. A seven match unbeaten run in November and December lifted them off the bottom of the table; but they immediately slumped again, losing eight of the next nine fixtures to drop back to the bottom. However, with Peter Beardsley and new signing Paul Goddard (from West Ham) linking well together up front, survival was secured with a nine match unbeaten run. They finished in 17th place, five points above relegated Leicester City. Goddard was the top scorer (with 11), while Neil McDonald contributed seven goals.

Chris Waddle's Spurs knocked Newcastle out of the F.A. Cup at the fifth round stage, while McFaul's side were the victims of Second Division Bradford City in the League Cup.

1987-1988 SEASON

After scoring 61 goals in 147 League games in his first spell on Tyneside, Peter Beardsley moved to Liverpool in the summer of 1987, for a record £1.9 million fee. His replacement was the Brazilian Mirandinha (whose profile soared when he scored against England in an international at Wembley).

With Mirandinha, Paul Goddard and Paul Gascoigne scoring most of the goals, Newcastle gradually moved into the top half of the table after a mediocre start. They finished 1987-88 with three successive wins to claim eighth spot. A late burst of scoring (10 goals as many games) by Michael O'Neill (who arrived from Coleraine) made him the top scorer with 12. Mirandinha netted 11 times, while Goddard scored eight goals. Neil McDonald was the only man to be ever-present.

Newcastle United slid out of both cups in 1987-88 to Wimbledon. They exited the League Cup in the third round at Plough Lane and, in the F.A. Cup, they lost to the eventual competition winners 3-1 at St James' Park in the fifth round.

1988-1989 SEASON

Paul Gascoigne (to Spurs for a record £2 million fee), Neil McDonald (to Everton) and Paul Goddard (to Derby County) had departed by the start of the 1988-89 campaign. Without them, United struggled, winning just one of their first seven fixtures. The board acted swiftly by sacking Willie McFaul. They tried to lure back Arthur Cox from Derby. However, their former boss resisted and remained at the Baseball Ground. Meanwhile at St James' Park, results went from bad to worse and goals were hard to come by.

Jim Smith joined as the new manager in early December. He immediately sold striker John Robertson back to Hearts after his failure to score (in 12 games) for the

Magpies and bought Kevin Brock from Queen's Park Rangers. Smith's arrival prompted two victories (from three games), but the club's failure to win more than three other fixtures meant that they were relegated in 20th and bottom place.

Mirandinha (in his last season on Tyneside) finished as the top scorer with nine goals out of a meagre total of 32 scored in the League. Nobody else contributed more than four goals. Among the other men to represent Newcastle United for the last time in 1988-89 were Ken Wharton (290 League appearances – 26 goals), David McCreery (243 – 2 goals) and Glenn Roeder (193 – 8 goals).

The Magpies exited the League Cup to Third Division Sheffield United in the second round. They also went out of the F.A. Cup at the first hurdle; but only after a marathon four encounters with Second Division Watford.

WILLIE McFAUL

Reign: 1985-1988
Honours: None
Highest League finish: 8th in 1987-88
Best F.A. Cup Run: Round 5 in 1986-87 and 1987-88
Best League Cup Run: Round 3 in 1987-88

1989-1990 SEASON

The arrival of Mick Quinn (from Portsmouth) added more punch to the attack in 1989-90. He weighed in with 32 goals (including four on his debut) and the returning Mark McGhee added a further 19 as Newcastle banged in 80 goals. However, Jim Smith's side only won one of their last four games to finish third, five points off an automatic promotion place, in a play-off position.

Newcastle United's promotion prospects looked bright after their play-off semi-final first leg when they held Sunderland to a goalless draw at Roker Park. However, it was the Wearsiders who had the better of the second leg, and their 2-0 victory was a real choker for the bulk of the 32,216 crowd.

The Magpies also experienced two cup defeats on their own ground earlier in the campaign. West Bromwich Albion beat them 1-0 in the League Cup and Manchester United won 3-2 in the fifth round of the F.A. Cup.

1990-1991 SEASON

After a promising start, Newcastle gradually drifted into the middle of the pack in 1990-91. Goals became hard to come by again and, despite a spell of just one defeat in nine games, Jim Smith resigned near the end of March. His replacement was former Argentinian midfielder Ossie Ardiles, who was manager of Swindon Town.

Newcastle finished in 11th place, with 18-goal Mick Quinn top scoring and Gavin Peacock contributing seven goals. John Anderson made his 299th and last League appearance (14 goals) for the Magpies in 1990-91. In contrast, on 10th November, Steve Watson made his debut at the tender age of 16 years and 223 days – to become the youngest man to represent the club in the League.

There was little cup joy in 1990-91, with Middlesbrough spinning Newcastle United out of the League Cup and Nottingham Forest proving too good for them in the F.A. Cup.

JIM SMITH

Reign: 1988-1991
Honours: None
Highest League finish: 20th
Best F.A. Cup Run: Round 5 in 1989-90
Best League Cup Run: Round 3 in 1989-90

1991-1992 SEASON

Ossie Ardiles' reign at the St James' Park helm only lasted 11 months. He was sacked following a 5-2 defeat at Oxford in February 1992. His side were then just one place off the bottom of the Second Division and had just leaked 15 goals in four games.

Kevin Keegan was the surprise, but extremely popular, choice to succeed the Argentinian. Despite a run of five defeats, Newcastle just survived relegation (by four points) in 20th place, by winning their last two games. Their leading scorer was Gavin Peacock with 16, while David Kelly contributed 11 goals.

Newcastle slipped out of both cups to Third Division opposition at the third round stage. Peterborough United put paid to their League Cup hopes and, in the F.A. Cup, Bournemouth showed the cooler nerves in a penalty shoot-out at St James' Park.

OSSIE ARDILES

Reign: 1991-1992
Honours: None
Highest League finish: 11th in Division Two in 1990-91
Best F.A. Cup Run: Round 3 in 1991-92
Best League Cup Run: Round 3 in 1991-92

1992-1993 SEASON

The Premier League kicked off in August 1992, but obviously without Newcastle United. However, with Sir John Hall finally gaining control of the club, serious money was now available for transfer dealing. Newcastle's ambitions were very apparent as Kevin Keegan recruited Barry Venison, John Beresford and Paul Bracewell during the close season.

Keegan's side set off at lightning pace, clocking up 11 straight League wins. Together with the two victories at the back-end of 1991-92, this formed a club record 13 League wins on the reel. Robert Lee, Scott Sellars and finally Andy Cole (for £1.75 million) were all added to the squad and the Magpies finished 1992-93 as the Football League champions with 96 points, a club record.

David Kelly top scored with 24, while Cole added 12 from the same number of appearances to be the joint second highest scorer (along with Gavin Peacock).

Newcastle defeated Mansfield Town and Middlesbrough before exiting the League Cup at Chelsea. They side-stepped Port Vale and Rotherham United in the F.A. Cup before losing by a single goal at Ewood Park.

1993-1994 SEASON

Kevin Keegan sold David Kelly to Wolves before the start of the 1993-94 campaign; but greatly strengthened his side when he enticed Peter Beardsley back to St James' Park. After a mixed start, the Magpies gained momentum and by December had reached the top three of the Premiership. With Andy Cole (34) and Beardsley (21) rattling in 55 goals between them, Newcastle maintained their marvellous form throughout the campaign. They won 10 out of the last 14 fixtures to secure third place and qualify for the UEFA Cup. It was the club's highest placing in the top-flight for 67 years, in fact since their most recent top-flight championship campaign of 1926-27.

Cole finished as the Premiership's leading scorer, although ironically he was not on the scoresheet when his side thumped Swindon Town 7-1. The Magpies also won 7-1 (11-2 on aggregate) at Notts County in the League Cup, when Cole claimed a hat-trick. However, Wimbledon knocked Newcastle out in the third round and second-flight Luton Town ended their F.A. Cup hopes in a fourth round replay.

Kevin Scott made his 229th and last League appearance (8 goals) for Newcastle United in 1993-94, before joining Tottenham Hotspur.

1994-1995 SEASON

The Magpies registered a flying 29 point start out of a possible 33 from their first 11 games of 1994-95, but were gradually weighed down by injuries to key players. After easily beating Royal Antwerp in the first round, Newcastle disappointingly slipped out of the UEFA Cup, on away goals, against Athletic Bilbao.

Kevin Keegan's side seemed to lose some of their confidence after their UEFA Cup exit. They drifted down the table and experienced a dire spell when they only won one of 11 League games. While the £7 million sale of Andy Cole to Manchester United, in early 1995, left them short of fire-power.

Newcastle gained revenge for their League Cup fourth round defeat by Manchester City, by beating the Citizens 3-1 at St James' Park in the F.A. Cup fifth round. Unfortunately, the Magpies were bundled out by a single Everton goal at Goodison Park in the next round. However, that 1994-95 quarter-final appearance represented the club's first for 19 years.

Keegan's side won only two of their final seven fixtures and had to settle for a very disappointing sixth place. Peter Beardsley was the leading goalscorer (with 13), while Ruel Fox netted 10 times.

1995-1996 SEASON

Newcastle United were knocked out of the F.A. Cup in 1995-96 by Chelsea, in a third round penalty shoot-out at St James' Park. They fared much better in the League Cup, knocking out Bristol City, Stoke City and Liverpool en route to the quarter-final stage. However, a 2-0 reverse at Arsenal signalled the end of the run.

The club's main priority in 1995-96 was the Premiership title and for much of the campaign they looked good bets, having led the table from the start through until the end of February. They won 13 out of their opening 19 League fixtures, losing just three times (at Southampton, Chelsea and Manchester United). During January they held a 12-point advantage over their main rivals (Liverpool and Manchester United) and did not drop a point a home until going down 1-0 to the Red Devils on 4th March.

Sadly, Keegan (who made an emotional outburst against Alex Ferguson) and his side cracked under the pressure of the fight. Even so, if Ferguson's Manchester United side (who held a two-point lead) had slipped up on the last Sunday and lost at Middlesbrough, Newcastle could still have nicked the title by winning at home to Tottenham. However, the Manchester side won 3-0 and Keegan's men were held to a 1-1 draw.

Newcastle United were the runners-up, four points adrift of the champions; but seven points clear of third placed Liverpool. Keegan's side only suffered eight League defeats (including a 4-3 thriller at Anfield) all term.

Les Ferdinand was the club's leading scorer (with 25), while Rob Lee and Peter Beardsley netted eight goals apiece. Shaka Hislop and Pavel Srnicek shared the goalkeeper's jersey, while Warren Barton, John Beresford, Lee Clark, Darren Peacock, Steve Howey, David Ginola, Keith Gillespie, Phillipe Albert and Steve Watson were also key members of the 1995-96 squad. The skilful Colombian Faustino Asprilla and England midfielder David Batty also made an impact at St James' Park after joining the club towards the end of the campaign.

1996-1997 SEASON

Kevin Keegan made just one signing during the summer of 1996. But the player concerned was a very special one in the shape of Alan Shearer. In return Blackburn Rovers received a World record £15 million fee.

The Newcastle-born striker experienced defeat in two of his first three games in black and white; but his new side bounced back with a stirring sequence of seven successive victories.

The last of these wins was a wonderful 5-0 battering of Manchester United at St James' Park. Unfortunately, that fine form disappeared just as quickly as it had arrived. Keegan's side won only one of the next nine League fixtures (and also went out of the League Cup at Middlesbrough) to slip to sixth place. They responded by thrashing

Spurs 7-1 and Leeds United 3-0, at St James' Park, in a five day spell at the turn of the year. But, after his side drew at Charlton in the F.A. Cup, Keegan shocked English football by sensationally announcing his resignation. He had been the club's manager for almost five years and during that time had considerably boosted both the spirit within the club and its profile nationwide. However, his number one target – a major piece of silverware – had eluded him.

The Newcastle board wanted Barcelona manager Bobby Robson to succeed Keegan, but he turned down their approach. So, instead, they appointed Kenny Dalglish, Shearer's former boss at Blackburn.

Newcastle exited the F.A. Cup at home to Nottingham Forest; but looked on course for a long run in the UEFA Cup after knocking out Hamstad, Ferencvaros and Metz. However, they found Monaco (who won 4-0 on aggregate) too strong for them over the two quarter-final meetings.

Under Dalglish's stewardship, the Magpies lost only two League games (one of which was another 4-3 reverse at Anfield), but were always considered outsiders to win the title. However, they did move through the field to finish in the runners-up berth, seven points behind Manchester United.

Shearer was the leading scorer (with 25), while Les Ferdinand contributed 16 goals. Apart the addition of Shearer and the emergence of Robbie Elliott (to become the first choice left-back), the Newcastle United squad that finished second during 1996-97 was virtually the same that held down the same position 12 months earlier.

KEVIN KEEGAN

Reign: 1992-1997
Honours: Division One championship
Highest League finish: 2nd in 1995-96
Best F.A. Cup Run: Quarter-final in 1994-95
Best League Cup Run: Quarter-final in 1995-96
Best European Run: UEFA Cup Round 4 in 1996-97

1997-1998 SEASON

Kenny Dalglish changed the squad around during the summer of 1997. The arrivals included goalie Shay Given, Alessandro Pistone, Stuart Pearce, Temuri Ketsbaia, Jon Dahl Tomasson and Ian Rush. Those leaving the club included Robbie Elliott (to Bolton Wanderers), David Ginola (to Spurs) and Lee Clark (to Sunderland). However, the club was rocked by the ankle injury Alan Shearer received in a pre-season game at Goodison Park. In the knowledge that he would be without Shearer until the new year, Dalglish made a late attempt to keep the Tottenham-bound Les Ferdinand at the club. However, Ferdinand did move on and so did Peter Beardsley (to Bolton) after making a total (in two spells) of 276 League appearances (108 goals). One more arrival, early in the season, was another ex-Liverpool player John Barnes.

Newcastle made a promising start, winning five of their first seven League fixtures, but their lack of fire-power soon became a major handicap and they found themselves stuck in mid-division. Only another six games (out of 31) ended in victory and they finished in 13th place. They only scored 35 goals, with Barnes netting six times to be the top scorer. Shearer did not return until mid-March.

Dalglish's side enjoyed greater success in the cups than the League in 1997-98. They reached the quarter-final of the League Cup (beating Hull City and Derby County), but lost 2-0 to Liverpool at St James' Park. They also reached the League stage of the European Cup by knocking out Croatia Zagreb in the second qualifying round.

The Magpies enjoyed a great night defeating Barcelona 3-2 at St James' Park and then, courtesy of two late John Beresford goals, drew away at Dynamo Kiev (in front of a massive 100,000 crowd). However, they lost home and away to PSV Eindhoven and also the return match with Barcelona. A home win over the group winners from Kiev only secured them third place in the table.

Dalglish's side did go all the way to the Final in the F.A. Cup. They side-stepped Everton, Stevenage Borough (at the second attempt), Tranmere Rovers, Barnsley and Sheffield United (in an Old Trafford semi-final) to meet Arsenal at Wembley. The Gunners were the better side on the day and wrapped up the 'Double' by scoring midway through each half.

The Newcastle players who took the field against Arsenal, on 16th May, were: Given, Pistone, Pearce, David Batty, Nikos Dabizas, Steve Howey, Rob Lee, Warren Barton, Ketsbaia, Gary Speed and Shearer. Steve Watson, Andreas Andersson and Barnes came on from the bench. Andersson, Dabizas and Speed had been brought in to boost the flagging squad during the second half of the campaign.

1998-1999 SEASON

Newcastle United opened the 1998-99 campaign with two draws. Then, on 27th August, the board sacked Kenny Dalglish and his assistant Terry McDermott. Ruud Gullit was immediately installed as the new manager.

Three successive victories lifted the Magpies to fourth place at the end of September; however, this was to be their seasonal high. Gullit's side gradually slipped down the table and, after failing to win any of their last seven fixtures, had to be content with 13th place. 14-goal Alan Shearer was the club's leading scorer, while Nolberto Solano netted six times in his first campaign at St James' Park.

Blackburn Rovers ended Newcastle's League Cup hopes in a penalty shoot-out at St James' Park, while Partizan Belgrade halted their European Cup Winners' Cup run in the first round (on the away goals rule).

Newcastle did enjoy one long cup run in 1998-99 when they went all the way to Wembley again in the F.A. Cup. Crystal Palace and Bradford City were defeated to earn Gullit's side the chance the exact revenge on Blackburn in the fifth round. A goal by Louis Saha gave the Magpies success at Ewood Park, in a replay. A memorable 4-1 triumph over Everton in the quarter-final and a 2-0 win over Spurs, in an Old Trafford semi-final, booked their place in the Final against Manchester United.

The Magpies' 13th F.A. Cup Final ended in a 2-0 defeat, with the Red Devils netting early in each half. Gullit selected five of the men who wore black & white in the Final 12 months before. They were Shearer, Rob Lee, Gary Speed, Nikos Dabizas and Temuri Ketsbaia. The rest of the 1998-99 F.A. Cup Final starting line-up was: goalkeeper Steve Harper, Andy Griffin, Didier Domi, Laurent Charvet, Dietmar Hamann and Solano. Duncan Ferguson, Silvio Maric and Stephen Glass all came off the bench, but none of them managed to change the course of the game.

KENNY DALGLISH

Reign: 1997-1998
Honours: None
Highest League finish: 2nd in 1996-97
Best F.A. Cup Run: Final 1997-98
Best League Cup Run: Quarter-final in 1997-98
Best European Run: European Champions League First Group Stage in 1997-98

1999-2000 SEASON

Newcastle United accepted a club record fee of £8 million for Dietmar Hamann during the summer of 1999. However, the man who sold the German, Ruud Gullit, was not to stay at St James' Park much longer himself. The Dutchman resigned on

28th August, stating his side's "poor results" and the "constant scrutiny of his private life". Gullit's spending in a year at St James' Park amounted to £32 million, with his side winning just 18 of 52 games.

Gullit's side collected just one point from the first five fixtures, his last match at the helm was a 2-1 defeat at Sunderland. The Newcastle United board finally got their man when County Durham-born Bobby Robson agreed to be the new manager.

The first victory of the campaign was a 8-0 hammering of Sheffield Wednesday, with Alan Shearer finding the net five times. Three more victories moved Robson's side up to mid-table before Christmas and a five-match unbeaten run at the end of the campaign allowed them to secure 11th place in the final table. Shearer was the leading scorer in 1999-2000, with 23 goals, while Gary Speed contributed nine goals and Duncan Ferguson found the net on six occasions.

First Division Birmingham City knocked the Magpies out of the League Cup, but they enjoyed a longer run in the UEFA Cup. They defeated CSKA Sofia, 4-2 on aggregate, in the first round. Then, followed up by beating FC Zurich 5-2, over two legs. Their fifth game in the competition was a 1-0 reverse against AS Roma in the Italian capital. Hopes were still high when the two sides resumed combat on Tyneside, but an excited crowd of 33,739 witnessed a goalless draw and Newcastle's exit.

For the third successive season, under a third different manager, Newcastle United reached the last four of the F.A. Cup. They defeated Spurs 6-1 (in a replay) and Sheffield United 4-1, at St James' Park. They won 2-1 at Blackburn and, at the quarter-final stage, triumphed 3-2 at Tranmere. For the third successive season, the Toon Army visited Wembley Stadium. Again their side stumbled and trains returned north full of deflated fans. Rob Lee netted an equaliser midway through the second half but Chelsea beat Newcastle 2-1 and later returned to the National Stadium to lift the cup.

RUUD GULLIT

Reign: 1998-1999
Honours: None
Highest League finish: 13th
Best F.A. Cup Run: Final in 1998-99
Best League Cup Run: Round 4 in 1998-99
Best European Run: European Cup Winners' Cup Round 1 in 1998-99

2000-2001 SEASON

Bobby Robson's side started 2000-01 quite brightly and sat among the top three in the early tables. They gradually drifted down the table and, despite losing 5-0 at Highbury, were still in sixth place after winning at Leeds in late January. However, with Alan Shearer side-lined, they won just three of their last 14 League fixtures and finished in 11th place again. Carl Cort and Nolberto Solano were the joint leading scorers (with six apiece), while Shearer, Kieron Dyer and Gary Speed each netted five times.

Newcastle went out of both domestic cup competitions in Birmingham. They reached the fourth round of the League Cup but lost 2-1 at St Andrew's. And, after being held by the Villans at St James' Park, they were bundled out 1-0 at Villa Park in a third round replay.

2001-2002 SEASON

With Alan Shearer regaining full fitness, the Magpies were a far tougher proposition in 2001-02. They lost only three times during the first half of the campaign and topped the table over Christmas. Unfortunately Bobby Robson's side were not quite good enough to sustain their challenge for the title and had to be content with a fourth place finish, 16 points behind champions Arsenal.

23-goal Shearer was the club's leading scorer, while Welsh international Craig Bellamy (in his first season at St James' Park after his move from Coventry City) contributed nine goals. Rob Lee made his 303rd League and last League appearance (44 goals) for the club in 2001-02.

Newcastle reached the quarter-final stage in both domestic cup competitions in 2001-02. They defeated Brentford, Barnsley and Ipswich Town before exiting the League Cup to Chelsea at Stamford Bridge. Robson's side defeated Crystal Palace, Peterborough United and Manchester City in the F.A. Cup; but saw their run halted by Arsenal in a replay at Highbury.

Earlier in the campaign, Newcastle United defeated Sporting Lokern and TSV 1860 Munich before exiting (on the away goals rule) to Troyes in the Intertoto Cup.

Bobby Robson's marvellous career in football was officially recognised during the summer of 2002 when he received a knighthood.

2002-2003 SEASON

Newcastle only played in two domestic cup ties in 2002-03, but, in contrast, participated in 14 European games. They were defeated by second-flight Wolves in the F.A. Cup and were tipped out of the League Cup by Everton. However, a 5-0 aggregate victory over Zeljeznicar Sarajevo in the third qualifying round earned Sir Bobby Robson's side six Group E games in the European Champions League.

The Magpies looked doomed after losing their first three games. However, remarkably, they bounced back to win their next three games. They defeated Juventus and Dynamo Kiev, on Tyneside, before winning 3-2 at Feyenoord. Craig Bellamy netted twice, including a last-gasp winner. That win secured second place (behind the Italians) in that first stage group and earned Newcastle six Group A games in the second stage.

Robson's men started badly again, losing 4-1 at home to Internazionale and then by 3-1 at Barcelona. Two 3-1 victories over Bayer Leverkusen put Newcastle back in contention, but, after drawing in Milan and losing 2-0 at home to Barcelona, they could only finish third and exited the competition.

In the Premiership, the Magpies sat as low as 19th place after only winning one of their first five fixtures. However, 18 of the next 26 fixtures ended in victory as Newcastle forced their way into the top three. Three successive defeats, including a 6-2 embarrassment at home to champions-elect Manchester United, killed off any hopes of them finishing any higher than third. Newcastle finished 14 points behind the champions and nine points behind runners-up Arsenal. Alan Shearer netted 17 times to be the club's leading scorer, while Bellamy and Nolberto Solano both scored seven goals.

2003-2004 SEASON

Newcastle United made a dreadful start to 2003-04, drawing three and losing three of the their opening six fixtures. However, the Magpies then found their true form and gradually climbed the table to lie in fifth place at Christmas. Sir Bobby Robson's side could not make any impact on the top three (Arsenal, Chelsea and Manchester United) who had drawn clear of the pack, but still had the chance of securing the fourth Champions League spot. Sadly, their failure to beat Wolves in their final home fixture meant that Newcastle could only finish as high as fifth. That position (and qualification for the UEFA Cup) was secured over the last two fixtures, with creditable away draws at Southampton and Liverpool.

Alan Shearer bagged 22 goals to be the club's leading scorer and was the second most lethal striker (behind Thierry Henry) in the Premiership in 2003-04. With Craig Bellamy missing nearly two-thirds of the season through injury, Newcastle's second top scorer was Shola Ameobi (seven goals), while Laurent Robert found the net six times. The ever-present Shay Given had another excellent campaign between the posts, while Jonathan Woodgate was easily the club's most impressive defender. Sadly, the former Leeds man missed half of the campaign through injury and lost the chance to represent his country in the European Championship in Portugal. Another injury-prone Magpie, Kieron Dyer, was selected by England for the summer tournament.

The Magpies had no joy in the League Cup, losing 2-1 at home to West Bromwich Albion (after extra-time). They did win 3-0 at Southampton in the F.A. Cup; but then went out 2-1 at Anfield, in the fourth round.

Newcastle's Champions League involvement lasted only two games, after losing on penalties to Partizan. So, instead, Robson's side focused on the UEFA Cup. NAC Breda, FC Basle, Vålerenga and Real Mallorca were all side-stepped en route to the quarter-final stage.

After drawing 1-1 against PSV in Eindhoven, the Magpies cemented a place in the last four by beating the Dutch side 2-1 at St James' Park. In the semi-final home leg, Newcastle were held to a goalless draw by Marseille. The Magpies gave their all in the second leg, in France, but crashed out of the competition by a 2-0 scoreline.

Newcastle United fans went into the summer of 2004 with high hopes. They had another UFEA Cup adventure to look forward to and, in the Premiership, had every reason to expect their side would make a serious bid for a top three place in 2004-05.

SIR BOBBY ROBSON

Reign: From 1999

Honours: None

Highest League finish: 3rd in 2002-03

Best F.A. Cup Run: Semi-final in 1999-2000

Best League Cup Run: Quarter-final in 2001-02

Best European Run: Champions League Second Group Stage in 2002-03 and UEFA Cup Semi-final in 2003-04

St James' Park as it looked during the late 1980s before recommendations of the Taylor Report led to all-seater Stadia.

The redevelopment of the ground after the Taylor Report means that St James' Park is now regarded as one of the best stadia in England seating over 52,000 fans on matchdays.

Season 1974/75

DIVISION ONE

Derby County	42	21	11	10	67	49	53
Liverpool	42	20	11	11	60	39	51
Ipswich Town	42	23	5	14	66	44	51
Everton	42	16	18	8	56	42	50
Stoke City	42	17	15	10	64	48	49
Sheffield United	42	18	13	11	58	51	49
Middlesbrough	42	18	12	12	54	40	48
Manchester City	42	18	10	14	54	54	46
Leeds United	42	16	13	13	57	49	45
Burnley	42	17	11	14	68	67	45
Queen's Park Rangers	42	16	10	16	54	54	42
Wolverhampton Wanderers	42	14	11	17	57	54	39
West Ham United	42	13	13	16	58	59	39
Coventry City	42	12	15	15	51	62	39
Newcastle United	**42**	**15**	**9**	**18**	**59**	**72**	**39**
Arsenal	42	13	11	18	47	49	37
Birmingham City	42	14	9	19	53	61	37
Leicester City	42	12	12	18	46	60	36
Tottenham Hotspur	42	13	8	21	52	63	34
Luton Town	42	11	11	20	47	65	33
Chelsea	42	9	15	18	42	72	33
Carlisle United	42	12	5	25	43	59	29

Season 1975/76

DIVISION ONE

Liverpool	42	23	14	5	66	31	60
Queen's Park Rangers	42	24	11	7	67	33	59
Manchester United	42	23	10	9	68	42	56
Derby County	42	21	11	10	75	58	53
Leeds United	42	21	9	12	65	46	51
Ipswich Town	42	16	14	12	54	48	46
Leicester City	42	13	19	10	48	51	45
Manchester City	42	16	11	15	64	46	43
Tottenham Hotspur	42	14	15	13	63	63	43
Norwich City	42	16	10	16	58	58	42
Everton	42	15	12	15	60	66	42
Stoke City	42	15	11	16	48	50	41
Middlesbrough	42	15	10	17	46	45	40
Coventry City	42	13	14	15	47	57	40
Newcastle United	**42**	**15**	**9**	**18**	**71**	**62**	**39**
Aston Villa	42	11	17	14	51	59	39
Arsenal	42	13	10	19	47	53	36
West Ham United	42	13	10	19	48	71	36
Birmingham City	42	13	7	22	57	75	33
Wolverhampton Wanderers	42	10	10	22	51	68	30
Burnley	42	9	10	23	43	66	28
Sheffield United	42	6	10	26	33	82	22

Season 1976/77

DIVISION ONE

Liverpool	42	23	11	8	62	33	57
Manchester City	42	21	14	7	60	34	56
Ipswich Town	42	22	8	12	66	39	52
Aston Villa	42	22	7	13	76	50	51
Newcastle United	**42**	**18**	**13**	**11**	**64**	**49**	**49**
Manchester United	42	18	11	13	71	62	47
West Bromwich Albion	42	16	13	13	62	56	45
Arsenal	42	16	11	15	64	59	43
Everton	42	14	14	14	62	64	42
Leeds United	42	15	12	15	48	51	42
Leicester City	42	12	18	12	47	60	42
Middlesbrough	42	14	13	15	40	45	41
Birmingham City	42	13	12	17	63	61	38
Queen's Park Rangers	42	13	12	17	47	52	38
Derby County	42	9	19	14	50	55	37
Norwich City	42	14	9	19	47	64	37
West Ham United	42	11	14	17	46	65	36
Bristol City	42	11	13	18	38	48	35
Coventry City	42	10	15	17	48	59	35
Sunderland	42	11	12	19	46	54	34
Stoke City	42	10	14	18	28	51	34
Tottenham Hotspur	42	12	9	21	48	72	33

Season 1977/78

DIVISION ONE

Nottingham Forest	42	25	14	3	69	24	64
Liverpool	42	24	9	9	65	34	57
Everton	42	22	11	9	76	45	55
Manchester City	42	20	12	10	74	51	52
Arsenal	42	21	10	11	60	37	52
West Bromwich Albion	42	18	14	10	62	53	50
Coventry City	42	18	12	12	75	62	48
Aston Villa	42	18	10	14	57	42	46
Leeds United	42	18	10	14	63	53	46
Manchester United	42	16	10	16	67	63	42
Birmingham City	42	16	9	17	55	60	41
Derby County	42	14	13	15	54	59	41
Norwich City	42	11	18	13	52	66	40
Middlesbrough	42	12	15	15	42	54	39
Wolverhampton Wanderers	42	12	12	18	51	64	36
Chelsea	42	11	14	17	46	69	36
Bristol City	42	11	13	18	49	53	35
Ipswich Town	42	11	13	18	47	61	35
Queen's Park Rangers	42	9	15	18	47	64	33
West Ham United	42	12	8	22	52	69	32
Newcastle United	**42**	**6**	**10**	**26**	**42**	**78**	**22**
Leicester City	42	5	12	25	26	70	22

Season 1978/79

DIVISION TWO

Crystal Palace	42	19	19	4	51	24	57
Brighton & Hove Albion	42	23	10	9	72	39	56
Stoke City	42	20	16	6	58	31	56
Sunderland	42	22	11	9	70	44	55
West Ham United	42	18	14	10	70	39	50
Notts County	42	14	16	12	48	60	44
Preston North End	42	12	18	12	59	57	42
Newcastle United	**42**	**17**	**8**	**17**	**51**	**55**	**42**
Cardiff City	42	16	10	16	56	70	42
Fulham	42	13	15	14	50	47	41
Orient	42	15	10	17	51	51	40
Cambridge United	42	12	16	14	44	52	40
Burnley	42	14	12	16	51	62	40
Oldham Athletic	42	13	13	16	52	61	39
Wrexham	42	12	14	16	45	42	38
Bristol Rovers	42	14	10	18	48	60	38
Leicester City	42	10	17	15	43	52	37
Luton Town	42	13	10	19	60	57	36
Charlton Athletic	42	11	13	18	60	69	35
Sheffield United	42	11	12	19	52	69	34
Millwall	42	11	10	21	42	61	32
Blackburn Rovers	42	10	10	22	41	72	30

Season 1979/80

DIVISION TWO

Leicester City	42	21	13	8	58	38	55
Sunderland	42	21	12	9	69	42	54
Birmingham City	42	21	11	10	58	38	53
Chelsea	42	23	7	12	66	52	53
Queen's Park Rangers	42	18	13	11	75	53	49
Luton Town	42	16	17	9	66	45	49
West Ham United	42	20	7	15	54	43	47
Cambridge United	42	14	16	12	61	53	44
Newcastle United	**42**	**15**	**14**	**13**	**53**	**49**	**44**
Preston North End	42	12	19	11	56	52	43
Oldham Athletic	42	16	11	15	49	53	43
Swansea City	42	17	9	16	48	53	43
Shrewsbury Town	42	18	5	19	60	53	41
Orient	42	12	17	13	48	54	41
Cardiff City	42	16	8	18	41	48	40
Wrexham	42	16	6	20	40	49	38
Notts County	42	11	15	16	51	52	37
Watford	42	12	13	17	39	46	37
Bristol Rovers	42	11	13	18	50	64	35
Fulham	42	11	7	24	42	74	29
Burnley	42	6	15	21	39	73	27
Charlton Athletic	42	6	10	26	39	78	22

Season 1980/81

DIVISION TWO

West Ham United	42	28	10	4	79	29	66
Notts County	42	18	17	7	49	38	53
Swansea City	42	18	14	10	64	44	50
Blackburn Rovers	42	16	18	8	42	29	50
Luton Town	42	18	12	12	61	46	48
Derby County	42	15	15	12	57	52	45
Grimsby Town	42	15	15	12	44	42	45
Queen's Park Rangers	42	15	13	14	56	46	43
Watford	42	16	11	15	50	45	43
Sheffield Wednesday	42	17	8	17	53	51	42
Newcastle United	**42**	**14**	**14**	**14**	**30**	**45**	**42**
Chelsea	42	14	12	16	46	41	40
Cambridge United	42	17	6	19	53	65	40
Shrewsbury Town	42	11	17	14	46	47	39
Oldham Athletic	42	12	15	15	39	48	39
Wrexham	42	12	14	16	43	45	38
Orient	42	13	12	17	52	56	38
Bolton Wanderers	42	14	10	18	61	66	38
Cardiff City	42	12	12	18	44	60	36
Preston North End	42	11	14	17	41	62	36
Bristol City	42	7	16	19	29	51	30
Bristol Rovers	42	5	13	24	34	65	23

Season 1981/82

DIVISION TWO

Luton Town	42	25	13	4	86	46	88
Watford	42	23	11	8	76	42	80
Norwich City	42	22	5	15	64	50	71
Sheffield Wednesday	42	20	10	12	55	51	70
Queen's Park Rangers	42	21	6	15	65	43	69
Barnsley	42	19	10	13	59	41	67
Rotherham United	42	20	7	15	66	54	67
Leicester City	42	18	12	12	56	48	66
Newcastle United	**42**	**18**	**8**	**16**	**52**	**50**	**62**
Blackburn Rovers	42	16	11	15	47	43	59
Oldham Athletic	42	15	14	13	50	51	59
Chelsea	42	15	12	15	60	60	57
Charlton Athletic	42	13	12	17	50	65	51
Cambridge United	42	13	9	20	48	53	48
Crystal Palace	42	13	9	20	34	45	48
Derby County	42	12	12	18	53	68	48
Grimsby Town	42	11	13	18	53	65	46
Shrewsbury Town	42	11	13	18	37	57	46
Bolton Wanderers	42	13	7	22	39	61	46
Cardiff City	42	12	8	22	45	61	44
Wrexham	42	11	11	20	40	56	44
Orient	42	10	9	23	39	61	39

Season 1982/83

DIVISION TWO

Queen's Park Rangers	42	26	7	9	77	36	85
Wolverhampton Wanderers	42	20	15	7	68	44	75
Leicester City	42	20	10	12	72	44	70
Fulham	42	20	9	13	64	47	69
Newcastle United	**42**	**18**	**13**	**11**	**75**	**53**	**67**
Sheffield Wednesday	42	16	15	11	60	47	63
Oldham Athletic	42	14	19	9	64	47	61
Leeds United	42	13	21	8	51	46	60
Shrewsbury Town	42	15	13	14	48	48	59
Barnsley	42	14	15	13	57	55	57
Blackburn Rovers	42	15	12	15	58	58	57
Cambridge United	42	13	12	17	42	60	51
Derby County	42	10	19	13	49	58	49
Carlisle United	42	12	12	18	68	70	48
Crystal Palace	42	12	12	18	43	52	48
Middlesbrough	42	11	15	16	46	67	48
Charlton Athletic	42	13	9	20	63	86	48
Chelsea	42	11	14	17	51	61	47
Grimsby Town	42	12	11	19	45	70	47
Rotherham United	42	10	15	17	45	68	45
Burnley	42	12	8	22	56	66	44
Bolton Wanderers	42	11	11	20	42	61	44

Season 1983/84

DIVISION TWO

Chelsea	42	25	13	4	90	40	88
Sheffield Wednesday	42	26	10	6	72	34	88
Newcastle United	**42**	**24**	**8**	**10**	**85**	**53**	**80**
Manchester City	42	20	10	12	66	48	70
Grimsby Town	42	19	13	10	60	47	70
Blackburn Rovers	42	17	16	9	57	46	67
Carlisle United	42	16	16	10	48	41	64
Shrewsbury Town	42	17	10	15	49	53	61
Brighton & Hove Albion	42	17	9	16	69	60	60
Leeds United	42	16	12	14	55	56	60
Fulham	42	15	12	15	60	53	57
Huddersfield Town	42	14	15	13	56	49	57
Charlton Athletic	42	16	9	17	53	64	57
Barnsley	42	15	7	20	57	53	52
Cardiff City	42	15	6	21	53	66	51
Portsmouth	42	14	7	21	73	64	49
Middlesbrough	42	12	13	17	41	47	49
Crystal Palace	42	12	11	19	42	52	47
Oldham Athletic	42	13	8	21	47	73	47
Derby County	42	11	9	22	36	72	42
Swansea City	42	7	8	27	36	85	29
Cambridge United	42	4	12	26	28	77	24

Season 1984/85

DIVISION ONE

Everton	42	28	6	8	88	43	90
Liverpool	42	22	11	9	68	35	77
Tottenham Hotspur	42	23	8	11	78	51	77
Manchester United	42	22	10	10	77	47	76
Southampton	42	19	11	12	56	47	68
Chelsea	42	18	12	12	63	48	66
Arsenal	42	19	9	14	61	49	66
Sheffield Wednesday	42	17	14	11	58	45	65
Nottingham Forest	42	19	7	16	56	48	64
Aston Villa	42	15	11	16	60	60	56
Watford	42	14	13	15	81	71	55
West Bromwich Albion	42	16	7	19	58	62	55
Luton Town	42	15	9	18	57	61	54
Newcastle United	**42**	**13**	**13**	**16**	**55**	**70**	**52**
Leicester City	42	15	6	21	65	73	51
West Ham United	42	13	12	17	51	68	51
Ipswich Town	42	13	11	18	46	57	50
Coventry City	42	15	5	22	47	64	50
Queen's Park Rangers	42	13	11	18	53	72	50
Norwich City	42	13	10	19	46	64	49
Sunderland	42	10	10	22	40	62	40
Stoke City	42	3	8	31	24	91	17

Season 1985/86

DIVISION ONE

Liverpool	42	26	10	6	89	37	88
Everton	42	26	8	8	87	41	86
West Ham United	42	26	6	10	74	40	84
Manchester United	42	22	10	10	70	36	76
Sheffield Wednesday	42	21	10	11	63	54	73
Chelsea	42	20	11	11	57	56	71
Arsenal	42	20	9	13	49	47	69
Nottingham Forest	42	19	11	12	69	53	68
Luton Town	42	18	12	12	61	44	66
Tottenham Hotspur	42	19	8	15	74	52	65
Newcastle United	**42**	**17**	**12**	**13**	**67**	**72**	**63**
Watford	42	16	11	15	69	62	59
Queen's Park Rangers	42	15	7	20	53	64	52
Southampton	42	12	10	20	51	62	46
Manchester City	42	11	12	19	43	57	45
Aston Villa	42	10	14	18	51	67	44
Coventry City	42	11	10	21	48	71	43
Oxford United	42	10	12	20	62	80	42
Leicester City	42	10	12	20	54	76	42
Ipswich Town	42	11	8	23	32	55	41
Birmingham City	42	8	5	29	30	73	29
West Bromwich Albion	42	4	12	26	35	89	24

Season 1986/87

DIVISION ONE

Everton	42	26	8	8	76	31	86
Liverpool	42	23	8	11	72	42	77
Tottenham Hotspur	42	21	8	13	68	43	71
Arsenal	42	20	10	12	58	35	70
Norwich City	42	17	17	8	53	51	68
Wimbledon	42	19	9	14	57	50	66
Luton Town	42	18	12	12	47	45	66
Nottingham Forest	42	18	11	13	64	51	65
Watford	42	18	9	15	67	54	63
Coventry City	42	17	12	13	50	45	63
Manchester United	42	14	14	14	52	45	56
Southampton	42	14	10	18	69	68	52
Sheffield Wednesday	42	13	13	16	58	59	52
Chelsea	42	13	13	16	53	64	52
West Ham United	42	14	10	18	52	67	52
Queen's Park Rangers	42	13	11	18	48	64	50
Newcastle United	**42**	**12**	**11**	**19**	**47**	**65**	**47**
Oxford United	42	11	13	18	44	69	46
Charlton Athletic	42	11	11	20	45	55	44
Leicester City	42	11	9	22	54	76	42
Manchester City	42	8	15	19	36	57	39
Aston Villa	42	8	12	22	45	79	36

Season 1987/88

DIVISION ONE

Liverpool	40	26	12	2	87	24	90
Manchester United	40	23	12	5	71	38	81
Nottingham Forest	40	20	13	7	67	39	73
Everton	40	19	13	8	53	27	70
Queen's Park Rangers	40	19	10	11	48	38	67
Arsenal	40	18	12	10	58	39	66
Wimbledon	40	14	15	11	58	47	57
Newcastle United	**40**	**14**	**14**	**12**	**55**	**53**	**56**
Luton Town	40	14	11	15	57	58	53
Coventry City	40	13	14	13	46	53	53
Sheffield Wednesday	40	15	8	17	52	66	53
Southampton	40	12	14	14	49	53	50
Tottenham Hotspur	40	12	11	17	38	48	47
Norwich City	40	12	9	19	40	52	45
Derby County	40	10	13	17	35	45	43
West Ham United	40	9	15	16	40	52	42
Charlton Athletic	40	9	15	16	38	52	42
Chelsea	40	9	15	16	50	68	42
Portsmouth	40	7	14	19	36	66	35
Watford	40	7	11	22	27	51	32
Oxford United	40	6	13	21	44	80	31

Season 1988/89

DIVISION ONE

Arsenal	38	22	10	6	73	36	76
Liverpool	38	22	10	6	65	28	76
Nottingham Forest	38	17	13	8	64	43	64
Norwich City	38	17	11	10	48	45	62
Derby County	38	17	7	14	40	38	58
Tottenham Hotspur	38	15	12	11	60	46	57
Coventry City	38	14	13	11	47	42	55
Everton	38	14	12	12	50	45	54
Queen's Park Rangers	38	14	11	13	43	37	53
Millwall	38	14	11	13	47	52	53
Manchester United	38	13	12	13	45	35	51
Wimbledon	38	14	9	15	50	46	51
Southampton	38	10	15	13	52	66	45
Charlton Athletic	38	10	12	16	44	58	42
Sheffield Wednesday	38	10	12	16	34	51	42
Luton Town	38	10	11	17	42	52	41
Aston Villa	38	9	13	16	45	56	40
Middlesbrough	38	9	12	17	44	61	39
West Ham United	38	10	8	20	37	62	38
Newcastle United	**38**	**7**	**10**	**21**	**32**	**63**	**31**

Season 1989/90

DIVISION TWO

Leeds United	46	24	13	9	79	52	85
Sheffield United	46	24	13	9	78	58	85
Newcastle United	**46**	**22**	**14**	**10**	**80**	**55**	**80**
Swindon Town	46	20	14	12	79	59	74
Blackburn Rovers	46	19	17	10	74	59	74
Sunderland	46	20	14	12	70	64	74
West Ham United	46	20	12	14	80	57	72
Oldham Athletic	46	19	14	13	70	57	71
Ipswich Town	46	19	12	15	67	66	69
Wolverhampton Wanderers	46	18	13	15	67	60	67
Port Vale	46	15	16	15	62	57	61
Portsmouth	46	15	16	15	62	65	61
Leicester City	46	15	14	17	67	79	59
Hull City	46	14	16	16	58	65	58
Watford	46	14	15	17	58	60	57
Plymouth Argyle	46	14	13	19	58	63	55
Oxford United	46	15	9	22	57	66	54
Brighton & Hove Albion	46	15	9	22	56	72	54
Barnsley	46	13	15	18	49	71	54
West Bromwich Albion	46	12	15	19	67	71	51
Middlesbrough	46	13	11	22	52	63	50
Bournemouth	46	12	12	22	57	76	48
Bradford City	46	9	14	23	44	68	41
Stoke City	46	6	19	21	35	63	37

Season 1990/91

DIVISION TWO

Oldham Athletic	46	25	13	8	83	53	88
West Ham United	46	24	15	7	60	34	87
Sheffield Wednesday	46	22	16	8	80	51	82
Notts County	46	23	11	12	76	55	80
Millwall	46	20	13	13	70	51	73
Brighton & Hove Albion	46	21	7	18	63	69	70
Middlesbrough	46	20	9	17	66	47	69
Barnsley	46	19	12	15	63	48	69
Bristol City	46	20	7	19	68	71	67
Oxford United	46	14	19	13	69	66	61
Newcastle United	**46**	**14**	**17**	**15**	**49**	**56**	**59**
Wolverhampton Wanderers	46	13	19	14	63	63	58
Bristol Rovers	46	15	13	18	56	59	58
Ipswich Town	46	13	18	15	60	68	57
Port Vale	46	15	12	19	56	64	57
Charlton Athletic	46	13	17	16	57	61	56
Portsmouth	46	14	11	21	58	70	53
Plymouth Argyle	46	12	17	17	54	68	53
Blackburn Rovers	46	14	10	22	51	66	52
Watford	46	12	15	19	45	59	51
Swindon Town	46	12	14	20	65	73	50
Leicester City	46	14	8	24	60	83	50
West Bromwich Albion	46	10	18	18	52	61	48
Hull City	46	10	15	21	57	85	45

Season 1991/92

DIVISION TWO

Ipswich Town	46	24	12	10	70	50	84
Middlesbrough	46	23	11	12	58	41	80
Derby County	46	23	9	14	69	51	78
Leicester City	46	23	8	15	62	55	77
Cambridge United	46	19	17	10	65	47	74
Blackburn Rovers	46	21	11	14	70	53	74
Charlton Athletic	46	20	11	15	54	48	71
Swindon Town	46	18	15	13	69	55	69
Portsmouth	46	19	12	15	65	51	69
Watford	46	18	11	17	51	48	65
Wolverhampton Wanderers	46	18	10	18	61	54	64
Southend United	46	17	11	18	63	63	62
Bristol Rovers	46	16	14	16	60	63	62
Tranmere Rovers	46	14	19	13	56	56	61
Millwall	46	17	10	19	64	71	61
Barnsley	46	16	11	19	46	57	59
Bristol City	46	13	15	18	55	71	54
Sunderland	46	14	11	21	61	65	53
Grimsby Town	46	14	11	21	47	62	53
Newcastle United	**46**	**13**	**13**	**20**	**66**	**84**	**52**
Oxford United	46	13	11	22	66	73	50
Plymouth Argyle	46	13	9	24	42	64	48
Brighton & Hove Albion	46	12	11	23	56	77	47
Port Vale	46	10	15	21	42	59	45

Season 1992/93

DIVISION ONE

Newcastle United	**46**	**29**	**9**	**8**	**92**	**38**	**96**
West Ham United	46	26	10	10	81	41	88
Portsmouth	46	26	10	10	80	46	88
Tranmere Rovers	46	23	10	13	72	56	79
Swindon Town	46	21	13	12	74	59	76
Leicester City	46	22	10	14	71	64	76
Millwall	46	18	16	12	65	53	70
Derby County	46	19	9	18	68	57	66
Grimsby Town	46	19	7	20	58	57	64
Peterborough United	46	16	14	16	55	63	62
Wolverhampton Wanderers	46	16	13	17	57	56	61
Charlton Athletic	46	16	13	17	49	46	61
Barnsley	46	17	9	20	56	60	60
Oxford United	46	14	14	18	53	56	56
Bristol City	46	14	14	18	49	67	56
Watford	46	14	13	19	57	71	55
Notts County	46	12	16	18	55	70	52
Southend United	46	13	13	20	54	64	52
Birmingham City	46	13	12	21	50	72	51
Luton Town	46	10	21	15	48	62	51
Sunderland	46	13	11	22	50	64	50
Brentford	46	13	10	23	52	71	49
Cambridge United	46	11	16	19	48	69	49
Bristol Rovers	46	10	11	25	55	87	41

Season 1993/94

F.A.PREMIERSHIP

Manchester United	42	27	11	4	80	38	92
Blackburn Rovers	42	25	9	8	63	36	84
Newcastle United	**42**	**23**	**8**	**11**	**82**	**41**	**77**
Arsenal	42	18	17	7	53	28	71
Leeds United	42	18	16	8	65	39	70
Wimbledon	42	18	11	13	56	53	65
Sheffield Wednesday	42	16	16	10	76	54	64
Liverpool	42	17	9	16	59	55	60
Queen's Park Rangers	42	16	12	14	62	61	60
Aston Villa	42	15	12	15	46	50	57
Coventry City	42	14	14	14	43	45	56
Norwich City	42	12	17	13	65	61	53
West Ham United	42	13	13	16	47	58	52
Chelsea	42	13	12	17	49	53	51
Tottenham Hotspur	42	11	12	19	54	59	45
Manchester City	42	9	18	15	38	49	45
Everton	42	12	8	22	42	63	44
Southampton	42	12	7	23	49	66	43
Ipswich Town	42	9	16	17	35	58	43
Sheffield United	42	8	18	16	42	60	42
Oldham Athletic	42	9	13	20	42	68	40
Swindon Town	42	5	15	22	47	100	30

Season 1994/95

F.A. PREMIERSHIP

Blackburn Rovers	42	27	8	7	80	39	89
Manchester United	42	26	10	6	77	28	88
Nottingham Forest	42	22	11	9	72	43	77
Liverpool	42	21	11	10	65	37	74
Leeds United	42	20	13	9	59	38	73
Newcastle United	**42**	**20**	**12**	**10**	**67**	**47**	**72**
Tottenham Hotspur	42	16	14	12	66	58	62
Queen's Park Rangers	42	17	9	16	61	59	60
Wimbledon	42	15	11	16	48	65	56
Southampton	42	12	18	12	61	63	54
Chelsea	42	13	15	14	50	55	54
Arsenal	42	13	12	17	52	49	51
Sheffield Wednesday	42	13	12	17	49	57	51
West Ham United	42	13	11	18	44	48	50
Everton	42	11	17	14	44	51	50
Coventry City	42	12	14	16	44	62	50
Manchester City	42	12	13	17	53	64	49
Aston Villa	42	11	15	16	51	56	48
Crystal Palace	42	11	12	19	34	49	45
Norwich City	42	10	13	19	37	54	43
Leicester City	42	6	11	25	45	80	29
Ipswich Town	42	7	6	29	36	93	27

Season 1995/96

F.A. PREMIERSHIP

Manchester United	38	25	7	6	73	35	82
Newcastle United	**38**	**24**	**6**	**8**	**66**	**37**	**78**
Liverpool	38	20	11	7	70	34	71
Aston Villa	38	18	9	11	52	35	63
Arsenal	38	17	12	9	49	32	63
Everton	38	17	10	11	64	44	61
Blackburn Rovers	38	18	7	13	61	47	61
Tottenham Hotspur	38	16	13	9	50	38	61
Nottingham Forest	38	15	13	10	50	54	58
West Ham United	38	14	9	15	43	52	51
Chelsea	38	12	14	12	46	44	50
Middlesbrough	38	11	10	17	35	50	43
Leeds United	38	12	7	19	40	57	43
Wimbledon	38	10	11	17	55	70	41
Sheffield Wednesday	38	10	10	18	48	61	40
Coventry City	38	8	14	16	42	60	38
Southampton	38	9	11	18	34	52	38
Manchester City	38	9	11	18	33	58	38
Queen's Park Rangers	38	9	6	23	38	57	33
Bolton Wanderers	38	8	5	25	39	71	29

Season 1996/97

F.A. PREMIERSHIP

Manchester United	38	21	12	5	76	44	75
Newcastle United	**38**	**19**	**11**	**8**	**73**	**40**	**68**
Arsenal	38	19	11	8	62	32	68
Liverpool	38	19	11	8	62	37	68
Aston Villa	38	17	10	11	47	34	61
Chelsea	38	16	11	11	58	55	59
Sheffield Wednesday	38	14	15	9	50	51	57
Wimbledon	38	15	11	12	49	46	56
Leicester City	38	12	11	15	46	54	47
Tottenham Hotspur	38	13	7	18	44	51	46
Leeds United	38	11	13	14	28	38	46
Derby County	38	11	13	14	45	58	46
Blackburn Rovers	38	9	15	14	42	43	42
West Ham United	38	10	12	16	39	48	42
Everton	38	10	12	16	44	57	42
Southampton	38	10	11	17	50	56	41
Coventry City	38	9	14	15	38	54	41
Sunderland	38	10	10	18	35	53	40
Middlesbrough	38	10	12	16	51	60	39
Nottingham Forest	38	6	16	16	31	59	34

Middlesbrough had 3 points deducted

Season 1997/98

F.A. PREMIERSHIP

Arsenal	38	23	9	6	68	33	78
Manchester United	38	23	8	7	73	26	77
Liverpool	38	18	11	9	68	42	65
Chelsea	38	20	3	15	71	43	63
Leeds United	38	17	8	13	57	46	59
Blackburn Rovers	38	16	10	12	57	52	58
Aston Villa	38	17	6	15	49	48	57
West Ham United	38	16	8	14	56	57	56
Derby County	38	16	7	15	52	49	55
Leicester City	38	13	14	11	51	41	53
Coventry City	38	12	16	10	46	44	52
Southampton	38	14	6	18	50	55	48
Newcastle United	**38**	**11**	**11**	**16**	**35**	**44**	**44**
Tottenham Hotspur	38	11	11	16	44	56	44
Wimbledon	38	10	14	14	34	46	44
Sheffield Wednesday	38	12	8	18	52	67	44
Everton	38	9	13	16	41	56	40
Bolton Wanderers	38	9	13	16	41	61	40
Barnsley	38	10	5	23	37	82	35
Crystal Palace	38	8	9	21	37	71	33

Season 1998/99

F.A. PREMIERSHIP

Manchester United	38	22	13	3	80	37	79
Arsenal	38	22	12	4	59	17	78
Chelsea	38	20	15	3	57	30	75
Leeds United	38	18	13	7	62	34	67
West Ham United	38	16	9	13	46	53	57
Aston Villa	38	15	10	13	51	46	55
Liverpool	38	15	9	14	68	49	54
Derby County	38	13	13	12	40	45	52
Middlesbrough	38	12	15	11	48	54	51
Leicester City	38	12	13	13	40	46	49
Tottenham Hotspur	38	11	14	13	47	50	47
Sheffield Wednesday	38	13	7	18	41	42	46
Newcastle United	**38**	**11**	**13**	**14**	**48**	**54**	**46**
Everton	38	11	10	17	42	47	43
Coventry City	38	11	9	18	39	51	42
Wimbledon	38	10	12	16	40	63	42
Southampton	38	11	8	19	37	64	41
Charlton Athletic	38	8	12	18	41	56	36
Blackburn Rovers	38	7	14	17	38	52	35
Nottingham Forest	38	7	9	22	35	69	30

Season 1999/2000

F.A. PREMIERSHIP

Manchester United	38	28	7	3	97	45	91
Arsenal	38	22	7	9	73	43	73
Leeds United	38	21	6	11	58	43	69
Liverpool	38	19	10	9	51	30	67
Chelsea	38	18	11	9	53	34	65
Aston Villa	38	15	13	10	46	35	58
Sunderland	38	16	10	12	57	56	58
Leicester City	38	16	7	15	55	55	55
West Ham United	38	15	10	13	52	53	55
Tottenham Hotspur	38	15	8	15	57	49	53
Newcastle United	**38**	**14**	**10**	**14**	**63**	**54**	**52**
Middlesbrough	38	14	10	14	46	52	52
Everton	38	12	14	12	59	49	50
Coventry City	38	12	8	18	47	54	44
Southampton	38	12	8	18	45	62	44
Derby County	38	9	11	18	44	57	38
Bradford City	38	9	9	20	38	68	36
Wimbledon	38	7	12	19	46	74	33
Sheffield Wednesday	38	8	7	23	38	70	31
Watford	38	6	6	26	35	77	24

Season 2000/2001

F.A. PREMIERSHIP

Manchester United	38	24	8	6	79	31	80
Arsenal	38	20	10	8	63	38	70
Liverpool	38	20	9	9	71	39	69
Leeds United	38	20	8	10	64	43	68
Ipswich Town	38	20	6	12	57	42	66
Chelsea	38	17	10	11	68	45	61
Sunderland	38	15	12	11	46	41	57
Aston Villa	38	13	15	10	46	43	54
Charlton Athletic	38	14	10	14	50	57	52
Southampton	38	14	10	14	40	48	52
Newcastle United	**38**	**14**	**9**	**15**	**44**	**50**	**51**
Tottenham Hotspur	38	13	10	15	47	54	49
Leicester City	38	14	6	18	39	51	48
Middlesbrough	38	9	15	14	44	44	42
West Ham United	38	10	12	16	45	50	42
Everton	38	11	9	18	45	59	42
Derby County	38	10	12	16	37	59	42
Manchester City	38	8	10	20	41	65	34
Coventry City	38	8	10	20	36	63	34
Bradford City	38	5	11	22	30	70	26

Season 2001/2002

F.A. PREMIERSHIP

Arsenal	38	26	9	3	79	36	87
Liverpool	38	24	8	6	67	30	80
Manchester United	38	24	5	9	87	45	77
Newcastle United	**38**	**21**	**8**	**9**	**74**	**52**	**71**
Leeds United	38	18	12	8	53	37	66
Chelsea	38	17	13	8	66	38	64
West Ham United	38	15	8	15	48	57	53
Aston Villa	38	12	14	12	46	47	50
Tottenham Hotspur	38	14	8	16	49	53	50
Blackburn Rovers	38	12	10	16	55	51	46
Southampton	38	12	9	17	46	54	45
Middlesbrough	38	12	9	17	35	47	45
Fulham	38	10	14	14	36	44	44
Charlton Athletic	38	10	14	14	38	49	44
Everton	38	11	10	17	45	57	43
Bolton Wanderers	38	9	13	16	44	62	40
Sunderland	38	10	10	18	29	51	40
Ipswich Town	38	9	9	20	41	64	36
Derby County	38	8	6	24	33	63	30
Leicester City	38	5	13	20	30	64	28

Season 2002/2003

F.A. PREMIERSHIP

Manchester United	38	25	8	5	74	34	83
Arsenal	38	23	9	6	85	42	78
Newcastle United	**38**	**21**	**6**	**11**	**63**	**48**	**69**
Chelsea	38	19	10	9	68	38	67
Liverpool	38	18	10	10	61	41	64
Blackburn Rovers	38	16	12	10	52	43	60
Everton	38	17	8	13	48	49	59
Southampton	38	13	13	12	43	46	52
Manchester City	38	15	6	17	47	54	51
Tottenham Hotspur	38	14	8	16	51	62	50
Middlesbrough	38	13	10	15	48	44	49
Charlton Athletic	38	14	7	17	45	56	49
Birmingham City	38	13	9	16	41	49	48
Fulham	38	13	9	16	41	50	48
Leeds United	38	14	5	19	58	57	47
Aston Villa	38	12	9	17	42	47	45
Bolton Wanderers	38	10	14	14	41	51	44
West Ham United	38	10	12	16	42	59	42
West Bromwich Albion	38	6	8	24	29	65	26
Sunderland	38	4	7	27	21	65	19

Season 2003/2004

F.A. PREMIERSHIP

Arsenal	38	26	12	0	73	26	90
Chelsea	38	24	7	7	67	30	79
Manchester United	38	23	6	9	64	35	75
Liverpool	38	16	12	10	55	37	60
Newcastle United	**38**	**13**	**17**	**8**	**52**	**40**	**56**
Aston Villa	38	15	11	12	48	44	56
Charlton Athletic	38	14	11	13	51	51	53
Bolton Wanderers	38	14	11	13	48	56	53
Fulham	38	14	10	14	52	46	52
Birmingham City	38	12	14	12	43	48	50
Middlesbrough	38	13	9	16	44	52	48
Southampton	38	12	11	15	44	45	47
Portsmouth	38	12	9	17	47	54	45
Tottenham Hotspur	38	13	6	19	47	57	45
Blackburn Rovers	38	12	8	18	51	59	44
Manchester City	38	9	14	15	55	54	41
Everton	38	9	12	17	45	57	39
Leicester City	38	6	15	17	48	65	33
Leeds United	38	8	9	21	40	79	33
Wolverhampton Wanderers	38	7	12	19	38	77	33

1974-75

1	Aug	17	(h)	Coventry C	W	3-2	Macdonald, Howard, Kennedy	35,950
2		21	(h)	Sheffield U	D	2-2	Macdonald, Burns	34,283
3		24	(a)	Wolverhampton W	L	2-4	Tudor 2	23,526
4		27	(a)	Sheffield U	L	1-2	Keeley	17,650
5		31	(h)	West Ham U	W	2-0	Tudor, Macdonald	30,782
6	Sep	7	(a)	Derby Co	D	2-2	Macdonald, Burns	21,197
7		14	(h)	Carlisle U	W	1-0	Tudor	40,568
8		21	(a)	QPR	W	2-1	Tudor, Burns	18,594
9		28	(h)	Ipswich T	W	1-0	Howard	43,526
10	Oct	5	(a)	Everton	D	1-1	McDermott	40,000
11		12	(h)	Stoke C	D	2-2	Tudor, Keeley	39,658
12		16	(h)	Wolverhampton W	D	0-0		30,825
13		19	(a)	Birmingham C	L	0-3		33,339
14		26	(h)	Leicester C	L	0-1		34,988
15	Nov	2	(h)	Luton T	W	1-0	Tudor	30,141
16		9	(a)	Middlesbrough	D	0-0		39,000
17		16	(h)	Chelsea	W	5-0	Cannell, Macdonald 2, Kennedy, Barrowclough	35,236
18		23	(a)	Burnley	L	1-4	Barrowclough	19,523
19		30	(h)	Manchester C	W	2-1	Macdonald, Howard	37,684
20	Dec	7	(a)	Tottenham H	L	0-3		23,422
21		14	(a)	Coventry C	L	0-2		15,562
22		21	(h)	Leeds U	W	3-0	Tudor, Kennedy, Howard	34,054
23		26	(a)	Carlisle U	W	2-1	Tudor, Macdonald	20,605
24	Jan	11	(h)	Tottenham H	L	2-5	Craig T, Burns	39,679
25		18	(a)	Manchester C	L	1-5	Macdonald	32,021
26	Feb	1	(h)	Middlesbrough	W	2-1	Macdonald, Burns	42,514
27		8	(a)	Luton T	L	0-1		18,019
28		12	(h)	Liverpool	W	4-1	Tudor, Macdonald 2, Barrowclough	38,115
29		15	(h)	Burnley	W	3-0	Macdonald 2, Barrowclough	40,602
30		22	(a)	Chelsea	L	2-3	Tudor, Macdonald	26,770
31		28	(a)	West Ham U	W	1-0	Macdonald	33,150
32	Mar	15	(a)	Ipswich T	L	4-5	Tudor 2, Macdonald 2	23,450
33		18	(a)	Arsenal	L	0-3		16,540
34		22	(h)	Derby Co	L	0-2		32,201
35		25	(a)	Liverpool	L	0-4		41,147
36		29	(a)	Leeds U	D	1-1	Nulty	41,225
37		31	(h)	QPR	D	2-2	Tudor, Macdonald	29,819
38	Apr	5	(a)	Leicester C	L	0-4		23,132
39		12	(h)	Everton	L	0-1		29,585
40		19	(a)	Stoke C	D	0-0		32,302
41		23	(h)	Arsenal	W	3-1	Bruce, Macdonald, Craig T	21,895
42		26	(h)	Birmingham C	L	1-2	Macdonald	24,787

FINAL LEAGUE POSITION: 15th in Division One

Appearances

Sub. Appearances

Goals

McFaul	Nattras	Kennedy	Smith	Keeley	Howard	Burns	Cassidy	Macdonald	Tudor	Hibbitt	Craig D	McDermott	Clark	Gibb	Barrowclough	Cannell	Bruce	Bell	Laughton	Nulty	Craig T	Barker	McCaffery	Blackhall	Crosson	Kelly	Hudson	Mahoney	
1	2	3*	4	5	6	7	8	9	10	11	12																		1
1	2	3	8	5	6	7		9	10	11			4																2
1	2*	3	8	5	6	7		9	10	11	12		4																3
1	8	3		5	6	7		9	10	11	2		4																4
1	8			5	6	7		9	10	11	2		4	3															5
1	2			5	6	7	8	9	10	11			3	4															6
1	2	12		5	6	7	8	9	10	11		4*	3																7
1	2			5	6	7		9	10	11			4	3	8														8
1	2			5	6	7		9	10	11			4	3	8														9
1	2	3		5	6	7		9	10	11			4		8														10
1	2	3		5	6	7*		9	10	11			4		8	12													11
1	2	3		5	6	7		9	10	11			4		8														12
1	2	3		5	6	7		9	10	11			4		8														13
1		3		5	6	7	12	9	10	11		4*	2		8														14
1	2	8		5	6		4	9	10	11				3		7													15
1	2	8		5	6		4	9	10	11				3		7													16
1	2	8	12	5	6		4	9		11*				3		7	10												17
1	2	8	11	5	6		4	9*	12					3		7	10												18
1		8	11*	5	6		4	9			2			3		7	10	12											19
	2	8			6	7		9						3	4		10	11	1	5									20
1	2	8		5	6	7		9	10					3		12	4	11*											21
1	2	8	11	5	6			9	10					3	4	7													22
1	2	3	4	5	6			9	10						7					8	11								23
1	2	3	4	5	6	7		9	10											8	11								24
1	2	3	4	5	6	7		9	10*						12					8	11								25
1	2	3	4	5	6	10		9							7					8	11								26
1		3	4	5		10		9				2	6		7					8	11								27
1	2	3	4	5	6			9	10						7					8	11								28
1	2	3	4	5	6			9	10						7					8	11								29
1	2	3*	4	5	6	12		9	10						7					8	11								30
1	6		4	5				9	10			2			7					8	11	3							31
1	6*		4					9	10			2	12		7					8	11	3	5						32
1			4					9	10			3			7					8	11		5	6	2				33
1			4	5	6			9	10			3			7					8	11					2			34
1			4*	5	6			9	10		2	3			7	12				8	11								35
1	2			5	6			9	10	4		3			7					8	11								36
1	2			5	6			9	10*	4		3			7	12				8	11								37
1	2			5	6			9				3			7	10*				8	11		12				4		38
	2			5				9		11	3		6	4	7*	10				8	12							1	39
		3		5	12			9		11	2*		6		7	10				8	4							1	40
1		3		5	6	7*		9		11		2	12			10				8	4								41
1		3		5	6			9		11		2			7	10				8	4								42
39	33	28	19	39	36	21	8	42	31	25	13	12	19	11	23	7	5	1	1	20	19	2	2	1	1	1	1	2	
			2		1	1	1		1		2		2	3		3					1	1							
		3		2	4	5		21	14			1			4	1	1				1	2							

1975-76

1	Aug	16	(a)	Ipswich T	W	3-0	Craig T (pen), Macdonald 2		27,680
2		20	(h)	Middlesbrough	D	1-1	Macdonald		41,417
3		23	(h)	Leicester C	W	3-0	Macdonald 2, Burns		36,084
4		27	(a)	Derby Co	L	2-3	Macdonald, Bruce		27,585
5		30	(a)	Manchester C	L	0-4			31,875
6	Sep	6	(h)	Aston Villa	W	3-0	Craig T, Macdonald 2		35,604
7		13	(a)	Everton	L	0-3			28,938
8		20	(h)	Wolverhampton W	W	5-1	Gowling 3, Tudor, Cassidy		30,876
9		23	(a)	Birmingham C	L	2-3	Craig T, Nulty		31,166
10		27	(a)	QPR	L	0-1			22,980
11	Oct	4	(h)	Tottenham H	D	2-2	Tudor, Barrowclough		33,284
12		11	(a)	West Ham U	L	1-2	Howard		30,400
13		18	(h)	Norwich C	W	5-2	Gowling 2, Macdonald 2, (og)		32,799
14		25	(a)	Stoke C	D	1-1	Gowling		24,057
15	Nov	1	(h)	Arsenal	W	2-0	Gowling, Nattrass		34,968
16		8	(a)	Leeds U	L	0-3			39,304
17		15	(h)	Liverpool	L	1-2	Nulty		41,145
18		22	(a)	Norwich C	W	2-1	Nulty 2		19,036
19		29	(a)	Manchester U	L	0-1			52,264
20	Dec	6	(h)	Coventry C	W	4-0	Craig T 2 (1 pen), Burns, Craig D		27,172
21		13	(a)	Leicester C	L	0-1			18,130
22		20	(h)	Ipswich T	D	1-1	Nulty		26,152
23		26	(a)	Burnley	W	1-0	Craig T (pen)		22,458
24		27	(h)	Sheffield U	D	1-1	Macdonald		31,762
25	Jan	10	(h)	Everton	W	5-0	Gowling 3, Nulty, Nattrass		31,726
26		17	(a)	Aston Villa	D	1-1	Gowling		36,389
27		31	(a)	Middlesbrough	D	3-3	Gowling, Kennedy, Nattrass		31,000
28	Feb	7	(h)	Derby Co	W	4-3	Craig T (pen), Macdonald, Nulty, (og)		45,770
29		21	(a)	Liverpool	L	0-2			43,404
30	Mar	3	(h)	Stoke C	L	0-1			38,822
31		13	(h)	West Ham U	W	2-1	Craig T (pen), Macdonald		33,866
32		16	(a)	Arsenal	D	0-0			18,424
33		20	(h)	Manchester U	L	3-4	Gowling, Macdonald, Burns		45,043
34		27	(a)	Coventry C	D	1-1	Bird		14,144
35		31	(h)	Leeds U	L	2-3	Craig T (pen), Gowling		32,685
36	Apr	3	(h)	QPR	L	1-2	Gowling		30,145
37		7	(h)	Birmingham C	W	4-0	Gowling, Macdonald 2, Burns		18,893
38		10	(a)	Wolverhampton W	L	0-5			20,083
39		14	(h)	Manchester C	W	2-1	Macdonald, Cassidy		21,095
40		17	(h)	Burnley	L	0-1			24,897
41		19	(a)	Sheffield U	L	0-1			18,906
42		24	(a)	Tottenham H	W	3-0	Macdonald 2, Burns		29,649

FINAL LEAGUE POSITION: 15th in Division One

Appearances

Sub. Appearances

Goals

Mahoney	Nattrass	Kennedy	Nulty	Howard	Hibbitt	Burns	Bruce	Macdonald	Gowling	Craig T	Barrowclough	Bird	Cassidy	Tudor	Keeley	Craig D	Blackwell	Cannell	Hudson	Jones	Oates	McCaffery	MacLean	
1	2	3	4	5	6	7	8	9	10	11														1
1	2	3	4	5	6	7	8*	9	10	11	12													2
1	2	3	4	5	6	7	8	9	10	11														3
1	2	3	4	5	6	7	8*	9	10	11	12													4
1	2	3	4	6		8		9	10	11	8	5												5
1	2	3	4	6		7		9	10	11		5	8											6
1	2	3	4	6		7			10	11	12	5	8	9*										7
1	2	3	4	6		7			10	11		5	8	9										8
1	2	3	4	6		7			10	11		5	8	9										9
1	2	3	11	6		7		9	10			5		8	4									10
1	2	3	4	6		7		9	10	11	12	5		8*										11
1	2	3	4	6		7		9	10	11		8	5											12
1	2	3	4	6		7		9	10	11		8				5								13
1	2	3	4	6		7*		9	10	11		8	12			5								14
1	2	3	4	6		7		9	10	11		8				5								15
1	2	3	4	6		7		9	10	11		8				5								16
1	2	3	4	6		7		9	10	11		8				5								17
1	2	3	4	6		7		9	10	11		8				5								18
1	2	3	4	6		7*		9	10	11		8		12		5								19
1	2	3	4	6		7		9	10	11		8				5								20
1	2	3	4	6		7		9	10	11		8				5								21
1	2	3	4	6		7		9	10	11		8				5								22
1	2	3	4	6		12		9	10	11			7	8*		5								23
1	2	3	4	6				9	10	11		8	7			5								24
1	2	3	4	6		8		9	10	11		5	7											25
1	2	3	4	6		7		9	10*	11	12	5	8											26
1	2	3	4	6		7		9	10	11			8		5									27
1	2	3	4	6		7		9	10	11					5	8								28
1	2	3		6		7		9	10	11			4	8	12	5*								29
1		3		6		7		9*		11			4	8		5	2	10	12					30
		3		6		7		9	10	11			4	8		5	2			1				31
		3		6		7		9	10	11			4	8		5	2			1				32
	2	3		6		7		9	10	11			4	8*		5				1	12			33
1	2	3	6*			7		9	10	11			4			5			12		8			34
1	2	3				7		9	10	11			4			5			8		6			35
1	2	3				7		9	10	11			4			5			8		6			36
1	2	3				7		9	10		11		4			5			8		6			37
1	2	3				7		9	10	12	11		4*			5			8		6			38
1	2	3				7		9	10	11		5*	4						8		6	12		39
1	2	3				7		9	10	11			4				12		8		6	5		40
	2	3				7		9	10	11			4						8	1	6*	5	12	41
	2	3				7		9	10	11			4							1	6	5	8	42
37	39	42	28	34	4	40	4	39	41	39	23	19	20	6	4	14	3	1	7	5	9	3	1	
						1					1	5	1		1	1			2		1	1	1	
	3	1	7	1		5	1	19	16	9	1	1	2	2		1								

1976-77

1	Aug	21	(h)	Derby Co	D	2-2	Craig T (pen), Hudson	35,927
2		25	(a)	Tottenham H	W	2-0	Burns, Barrowclough	24,022
3		28	(h)	Bristol C	D	0-0		31,775
4	Sep	4	(a)	Middlesbrough	L	0-1		26,000
5		11	(h)	Manchester U	D	2-2	Burns, Cannell	39,037
6		18	(a)	Leeds U	D	2-2	Cannell, Cassidy	35,098
7		25	(h)	Liverpool	W	1-0	Cannell	34,813
8	Oct	2	(a)	Norwich C	L	2-3	Craig T (pen), Gowling	21,417
9		6	(h)	West Brom A	W	2-0	Gowling, Cannell	28,746
10		16	(a)	Coventry C	D	1-1	Gowling	18,083
11		23	(h)	Birmingham C	W	3-2	Craig T, Burns 2	31,711
12		30	(h)	Stoke C	W	1-0	Cannell	32,339
13	Nov	6	(a)	Manchester C	D	0-0		40,049
14		20	(a)	West Ham U	W	2-1	Burns, Nulty	21,324
15		24	(h)	Everton	W	4-1	Craig T, Gowling 2, Cannell	31,203
16		27	(h)	QPR	W	2-0	Burns, Cannell	39,045
17	Dec	4	(a)	Arsenal	L	3-5	Gowling, Burns 2	35,000
18		18	(a)	Aston Villa	L	1-2	Gowling	33,982
19		27	(h)	Sunderland	W	2-0	Cannell, Kennedy	49,644
20	Jan	22	(a)	Derby Co	L	2-4	Craig T (pen), Gowling	23,036
21	Feb	5	(a)	Bristol C	D	1-1	Burns	28,000
22		16	(h)	Manchester C	D	2-2	Burns 2	28,954
23		19	(a)	Manchester U	L	1-3	Nulty	51,828
24		26	(h)	Tottenham H	W	2-0	Gowling, Burns	30,230
25	Mar	2	(h)	Leeds U	W	3-0	Burns, Oates, McCaffery	33,714
26		5	(a)	Liverpool	L	0-1		45,553
27		9	(h)	Ipswich T	D	1-1	Nattrass	33,820
28		12	(h)	Norwich C	W	5-1	Craig T, Gowling, Oates, McCaffery 2	27,808
29		15	(a)	Stoke C	D	0-0		12,708
30		19	(a)	West Brom A	D	1-1	Barrowclough	23,780
31		23	(h)	Coventry C	W	1-0	Burns	25,332
32		26	(h)	Middlesbrough	W	1-0	Kennedy	33,643
33	Apr	2	(a)	Birmingham C	W	2-1	Craig T (pen), Barrowclough	20,283
34		8	(a)	Sunderland	D	2-2	Craig T, Cannell	50,048
35		9	(h)	Leicester C	D	0-0		32,300
36		16	(h)	West Ham U	W	3-0	Gowling, Cannell Nulty	30,967
37		23	(a)	QPR	W	2-1	Barrowclough, Nattrass	20,544
38		30	(h)	Arsenal	L	0-2		44,677
39	May	3	(a)	Leicester C	L	0-1		14,289
40		7	(a)	Ipswich T	L	0-2		24,760
41		14	(h)	Aston Villa	W	3-2	Cannell 2, Oates	29,873
42		24	(a)	Everton	L	0-2		25,208

FINAL LEAGUE POSITION: 5th in Division One

Appearances

Sub. Appearances

Goals

Mahoney	Nattrass	Kennedy	Hudson	Bird	Nulty	Barrowclough	Oates	Burns	Gowling	Craig T	Blackhall	Cannell	Tudor	Howard	McCaffrey	Cassidy	Craig D	Guy	Mitchell	
1	2	3	4	5	6	7	8	9	10	11										1
1	2	3	4	5	6	7	8	9*	10	11	12									2
1	2	3	4	5	6	7	8			11*		9	10	12						3
1	2	3	4		6	7		9	10	11*		12			5	8				4
1	2	3			6	7		9	10	11		8			5	4				5
1	2	3			6	7	10	9		11		8			5	4				6
1	2	3			6	7	10	9		11	12	8			5		4*			7
1	2	3			6	7		9	10	11		8			5	4				8
1	2*	3			6	7	12	9	10	11		8			5	4				9
1	2	3			6	7		9	10	11		8			5	4				10
1	2	3*			6	7		9	10	11	12	8			5	4				11
1	2	3			6	7		9		11		8			5	4	10			12
1	2	3			6	7		9	10	11		8			5	4				13
1	2	3			6	7		9	10	11		8			5	4				14
1	2	3*			6	7		9	10	11		8			5	4	12			15
1	2	3			6	7		9	10	11		8			5	4				16
1	2	3			6	7		9	10	11		8			5	4				17
1	2	3			6	7		9	10	11		8			5	4				18
1	2	3			6	7		9	10	11		8			5	4				19
1	2	3			6	7		9	10	11		8			5	4				20
1	2	3			6	7	12	9	10		11	8*			5	4				21
1	2	3			6	7		9	10	11					5	4		8		22
1	2	3			6	7		9	10	11					5	4		8		23
1	2	3			6	7*	12	9	10	11					5	4		8		24
1	2	3			6	7	8	9	10	11					5	4				25
1	2	3			6	7	8	9	10	11	12				5	4*				26
1	2	3			6	7	8	9	10	11		4			5					27
1	2	3			6	7	8	9	10	11		4			5					28
1	2	3			6	7	8	9	10	11					5	4				29
1	2	3			6	7		9	10*	11	12				5	4	8			30
1	2	3			6	7		9	10*	11	12	8			5	4				31
1	2	3			6	7		9	10	11		8			5	4				32
1	2	3			6	7		9	10	11		8			5	4				33
1	2	3			6	7		9	10	11		8			5	4				34
1	2	3			6	7		9	10	11	8				5	4				35
1	2	3			6	7		9	10	11	12	8			5	4*				36
1	2	3			6	7		9	10*	11	12	8			5	4*				37
1	2	3			6	7		9	10	11	12	8			5	4*				38
1	2*	3	12		6	7		9		11	10	8			5	4				39
1		3			6	7	10	9		11	2	8			5	4				40
1	2*	3			6		7	9	10	11	12	8			5	4				41
1		3		5	6	4	7	9	10	11		8								42
42	40	42	4	4	42	41	13	41	36	40	7	29	1		38	35	2	2	3	
			1				3			10	1			1			1			
	2	2	1		3	4	3	14	11	8		12			3	1				

37

1977-78

#	Month	Date		Opponent	Result	Score	Scorers	Attendance
1	Aug	20	(h)	Leeds U	W	3-2	Burns 2, Kennedy	36,700
2		23	(a)	Liverpool	L	0-2		48,267
3		27	(a)	Middlesbrough	L	0-2		26,712
4	Sep	3	(h)	West Ham U	L	2-3	Burns, Cassidy	26,942
5		10	(h)	West Brom A	L	0-3		22,705
6		17	(a)	Birmingham C	L	0-3		18,953
7		24	(h)	Coventry C	L	1-2	Gowling	22,484
8	Oct	1	(a)	Ipswich T	L	1-2	McCaffery	21,797
9		5	(a)	Norwich C	L	1-2	Craig T	16,630
10		8	(h)	Derby Co	L	1-2	Burns	26,578
11		15	(a)	Manchester U	L	2-3	Martin, Burns	55,056
12		22	(h)	Chelsea	W	1-0	Burns	23,683
13		29	(a)	Everton	D	4-4	Craig T, Gowling 2, Cassidy	37,574
14	Nov	5	(h)	Bristol C	D	1-1	Martin	23,321
15		12	(a)	Wolverhampton W	L	0-1		16,964
16		19	(h)	Arsenal	L	1-2	Cassidy	23,679
17	Dec	3	(h)	Leicester C	W	2-0	Burns, Nattrass	20,112
18		10	(a)	QPR	W	1-0	Robinson	15,251
19		17	(h)	Wolverhampton W	W	4-0	Craig T, Mitchell, Cassidy, Nattrass	22,982
20		26	(a)	Manchester C	L	0-4		45,811
21		28	(h)	Nottingham F	L	0-2		41,612
22		31	(h)	Liverpool	L	0-2		36,499
23	Jan	2	(a)	Leeds U	W	2-0	Burns 2	36,643
24		14	(h)	Middlesbrough	L	2-4	McGhee, Cassidy	34,460
25		21	(a)	West Ham U	L	0-1		25,461
26	Feb	25	(h)	Ipswich T	L	0-1		22,264
27	Mar	4	(a)	Derby Co	D	1-1	Burns	19,708
28		11	(h)	Manchester U	D	2-2	McGhee, Burns (pen)	25,825
29		15	(h)	Birmingham C	D	1-1	Nattrass	19,493
30		18	(a)	Chelsea	D	2-2	McGhee, Burns (pen)	22,777
31		24	(h)	Everton	L	0-2		28,933
32		25	(a)	Nottingham F	L	0-2		35,552
33		29	(h)	Manchester C	D	2-2	Bird, Kennedy	20,256
34	Apr	1	(a)	Bristol C	L	1-3	Barrowclough	17,344
35		4	(a)	Coventry C	D	0-0		22,135
36		8	(h)	Aston Villa	D	1-1	Burns (pen)	19,330
37		12	(a)	West Brom A	L	0-2		17,053
38		15	(a)	Arsenal	L	1-2	Burns	33,353
39		19	(a)	Aston Villa	L	0-2		25,495
40		22	(h)	QPR	L	0-3		13,463
41		26	(h)	Norwich C	D	2-2	Burns, Kennedy	7,986
42		29	(a)	Leicester C	L	0-3		11,530

FINAL LEAGUE POSITION: 21st in Division One

Appearances

Sub. Appearances

Goals

No	Mahoney	Nattrass	Kennedy	Cassidy	McCaffery	Bird	Barrowclough	Cannell	Burns	Gowling	Craig T	Hardwick	Blackwell	Oates	MacLean	Mitchell	Craig D	Callachan	Blackley	Kelly	Martin	Nulty	Barker	Walker	Smith	Robinson	Carr	Hudson	Gorry	Larnach	Barton	McGhee	Parkinson	Scott	Guy	No
1	1	2	3	4	5	6	7	8	9	10	11																									1
2		2	3	4	5	6	7	8*	9	10	11	1	12																							2
3		2*	3	4	5	6	7		9	10	11	1	12	8																						3
4	1	12	3	4	5	6			9		11		2	10	7	8*																				4
5	1	6	3		5	7	8		9	10*	11		4	12			2																			5
6	1	6	3		5	7	8		9		11		12	4*			2	10																		6
7	1	6	3	5		7			9	10	11		12	4*			2	8																		7
8	1	6	3	5		7			9	10	11		12	8			2*	4																		8
9	1	6	3	5		7			9	10	11		2	12	4			8*																		9
10	1	2		5		7			9	10*	11		3	8	4				6	12																10
11					5	4*	7	8	9		11	1	3			12			6	2	10															11
12		3	4		5		7	8	9	10	11	1								2	6															12
13		2	4		5		7		9	10	11	1							3	8	6															13
14		2			5		7		9	10	11	1							6		8		3	4												14
15		6	4		5		7		9		11	1				2					8		3	10*	12											15
16		6	4		5		7		9	10*	11	1				2				12			3	8												16
17		2	4		5			8		10		1		9					6		7		3			11										17
18		2	4		5			9	8*	10		1							6		7		3			11	1	12								18
19		2	4		5				8	10		1				9			6		7		3			11	1									19
20		2	4		5			9	8	10									6*		7		3			11	1		12							20
21		2	4		5		12	9*	8	10				6							7		3			11	1									21
22		2		5			7*		8	10				6						12			3			11	1	4		9						22
23			4	5			12		8		11			2									3				1	7		9	6*	10				23
24		6	4	5					8	10	11			2									3*		12		1	7				9				24
25	1	2	6	4*	5		11		7	12													3					8		10		9				25
26	1	2	10	4	5				8		11								6				3							9						26
27	1	4	3		5	7			8										6		2		12	11						9		10*				27
28	1	4	3		5	7*			8										6		2			11						9		10	12			28
29	1	4	3		5				8										6		2			11*		7				9		10	12			29
30	1	2	3		5				8										6*	12				11						9	4	10		7		30
31	1	2	3		5		12		8*													6		11						9	4	10		7		31
32	1	2	3		5	7										9						6		11							4	10				32
33	1	2	3		5	7			8							9						6		11							4	10				33
34	1	2	3		5*	7			8					6								9		11							4	10	12			34
35	1	5	3			7			8					2				10				6									4	9		11		35
36	1	5	3			7			8					2				10*				6								12	4	9		11		36
37	1	5	3		12	7			8					2		6		10													4	9		11*		37
38	1	5	3			7			8					2					6		10										4	9		11		38
39	1	5	3			7			8					2		9			6		10										4			11		39
40	1	2	3			7			8							9		5					6	11*						10	4	12				40
41		3				7			8							6		5		2				11			1			10	4	9				41
42									8				3			6		11		2		5	12				1			10	4	9*			7	42
	24	37	26	17	14	25	30	9	41	14	24	9	14	4	6	8	6	9	18	7	9	11	14	14	1	7	9	4		12	14	17		7	1	
		1			1	3			1					2	5	1				2	2		1		1	1		1	1	1		1	2	1		
		3	3	5	1	1	1		15	3	3					1				2						1						3				

39

1978-79

1	Aug	19	(a)	Millwall	L	1-2	Barton	12,105
2		23	(h)	West Ham U	L	0-3		27,167
3		26	(h)	Luton T	W	1-0	Pearson	24,112
4	Sep	2	(a)	Cambridge U	D	0-0		8,174
5		9	(h)	Blackburn R	W	3-1	Withe 2, McGhee	23,751
6		16	(a)	Wrexham	D	0-0		14,091
7		23	(h)	Orient	D	0-0		26,361
8		30	(a)	Notts Co	W	2-1	Connolly, Bird	11,362
9	Oct	7	(h)	Leicester C	W	1-0	Walker	25,731
10		14	(a)	Sunderland	D	1-1	Withe	35,405
11		21	(a)	Charlton Ath	L	1-4	Walker	11,616
12		28	(h)	Cardiff C	W	3-0	Connolly, Withe, Robinson	23,477
13	Nov	4	(a)	Bristol R	L	0-2		10,582
14		11	(h)	Millwall	W	1-0	Pearson	23,087
15		18	(a)	Luton T	L	0-2		10,434
16		22	(h)	Cambridge U	W	1-0	Bird	20,004
17		25	(h)	Oldham Ath	D	1-1	McGhee	20,563
18	Dec	2	(a)	Crystal Palace	L	0-1		19,761
19		9	(h)	Stoke C	W	2-0	Connolly, White	23,459
20		16	(a)	Fulham	W	3-1	Connolly, Withe, Shoulder	8,575
21		23	(h)	Burnley	W	3-1	Withe, Shoulder, Cassidy	23,639
22		26	(a)	Sheffield U	L	0-1		23,200
23		30	(a)	Brighton & HA	L	0-2		25,812
24	Feb	3	(a)	Orient	L	0-2		7,251
25		17	(a)	Leicester C	L	1-2	Nattrass	15,106
26		24	(h)	Sunderland	L	1-4	Connolly	34,733
27	Mar	3	(h)	Charlton Ath	W	5-3	Connolly, Shoulder 2 (1 pen), Martin, Mitchell	14,998
28		10	(a)	Cardiff C	L	1-2	Connolly	11,368
29		24	(a)	West Ham U	L	0-5		24,651
30		31	(a)	Oldham Ath	W	3-1	Withe, Shoulder (pen), Nattrass	6,329
31	Apr	4	(h)	Preston NE	W	4-3	Connolly, Withe, Shoulder, Barton	12,167
32		7	(h)	Crystal Palace	W	1-0	Shoulder	18,862
33		10	(a)	Burnley	L	0-1		7,851
34		14	(h)	Sheffield U	L	1-3	Shoulder	19,126
35		16	(a)	Preston NE	D	0-0		12,960
36		18	(h)	Notts Co	L	1-2	Withe	12,017
37		21	(h)	Fulham	D	0-0		11,924
38		25	(a)	Blackburn R	W	3-1	Withe 3	4,902
39		28	(a)	Stoke C	D	0-0		23,217
40	May	2	(h)	Bristol R	W	3-0	Withe, Shoulder, Bird	9,627
41		5	(h)	Brighton & HA	L	1-3	Shoulder	28,434
42		8	(h)	Wrexham	W	2-0	Peason, Shoulder	7,134

FINAL LEAGUE POSITION: 5th in Division Two

Appearances

Sub. Appearances

Goals

	Mahoney	Kelly	Barker	Cassidy	Bird	Barton	Walker	Pearson	Mitchell	Hibbitt	Connolly	Blackley	Suggett	Withe	Hardwick	Brownlie	McGhee	Nattrass	Scott	Robinson	Nicholson	Martin	Shoulder	Mulgrove	Guy	Parkinson	Wharton	Carr	Manners	
1	1	2	3	4	5	6	7	8	9	10	11																			1
2	1	2	3	4	5		7	9		10	11	6	8																	2
3	1	2	3	4	5			8		10	11	6	7	9																3
4		2		4	5	6		8		10	11		7	9	1	3														4
5		2		4*	5			8		10	11	6	7	9	1	3	12													5
6		2		4	5				12	10	11	6	7	9	1	3	8*													6
7		2		4					12	10	11	6*	7	9	1	3	8	5												7
8		2			5				12	10	11	6	7	9	1	3	8*		4											8
9		2*			5		8		4	10	11	6	7	9	1	3	12													9
10		2			5	6	8		4	10	11		7	9	1	3														10
11		2			5	6	8	7*	4	10			12	9	1	3	11													11
12		2			5		8			10	11	6	7	9	1	3	12	4*												12
13		2			5		8	4		10	11	6	7	9	1	3														13
14		2			5		8	4*		10	11	6	7	9	1	3	12													14
15		2*			5		8		4	10	11	6	7	9	1	3	12													15
16			3		5		8			10		6	7*	9	1	2	12	4				11								16
17			3		5		8		12	10		6		9	1	2	7	4*				11								17
18					5		8*		3	10	11	6	7	9	1	2		12				4								18
19				7	5				3	10	11	6		9	1	2						4	8							19
20				8	5	12			3	10	11	6*		9	1	2						4	7							20
21			12	8	5				3	10	11	6		9	1	2						4	7							21
22				8			5		3	10	11	6		9	1	2						4	7							22
23				8			5		3	10	11	6*		9	1	2						4	7	12						23
24					5				3	10		6		9	1	2		8		11*		4	7	12						24
25					5		12		3			6		9	1	2		8	10	11*		4	7							25
26					5		8		12	10	11	6*		9	1	2		3				4	7							26
27					5		8		3	10	11			9	1	2		6				4*	7			12				27
28					5		8		3	10	11		12	9	1	2		6				4	7*							28
29					5		8*		3	10	11			9	1	2		6				4	7				12			29
30				8	5				3	10	11			9	1	2		6				4	7							30
31				8			5			10	11	3		9	1	2		6				4	7							31
32				8			5			10	11	3		9	1	2		6				4	7							32
33				8			5			10	11	3		9	1	2		6				4	7							33
34				8					5	10	11	3		9	1	2		6				4	7							34
35				8			12		5	10	11	3		9		2		6				4*	7					1		35
36				8			4		5	10	11*	3	12	9		2		6					7					1		36
37				3	5	10		9					8			2*		6			11	4	7				12	1		37
38				6	5				3	10				8	9			2			11	4	7					1		38
39				6	5				3	10				8	9			2			11	4	7					1		39
40				6	5				3*	10	11			8	9			2				12	7					1	4	40
41				6	5				3*	10	11				9			2				12	8	7				1	4	41
42				6	5		8		3	10	11				9			2				4	7					1		42
	3	15	5	19	27	21	18	9	26	40	34	28	20	39	31	34	4	21	2	4	5	23	24					8	2	
		1			1	2		5					3				6					3		1	1	1	2			
				1	3	2	2	3	1		8		14				2	2			1	1	11							

1979-80

1	Aug	18	(h)	Oldham Ath	W	3-2	Withe, Shoulder 2 (2 pens)	19,099
2		21	(a)	Preston NE	L	0-1		12,707
3		25	(a)	Charlton Ath	D	1-1	Cassidy	6,849
4	Sep	1	(h)	Chelsea	W	2-1	Withe 2	25,047
5		8	(a)	Orient	W	4-1	Cartwright, Hibbitt, Withe, Shoulder (pen)	5,700
6		15	(h)	Leicester C	W	3-2	Cartwright, Shoulder 2 (2 pens)	26,443
7		22	(h)	Wrexham	W	1-0	Shoulder (pen)	27,904
8		29	(a)	Birmingham C	D	0-0		19,967
9	Oct	6	(a)	West Ham U	D	1-1	Withe	23,206
10		10	(h)	Preston NE	D	0-0		25,154
11		13	(h)	Shrewsbury T	W	1-0	Shoulder	21,603
12		20	(a)	Watford	L	0-2		17,715
13		27	(h)	Cambridge U	W	2-0	Withe, Shoulder	24,104
14	Nov	3	(a)	Oldham Ath	L	0-1		11,486
15		10	(h)	Cardiff C	W	1-0	Shoulder	22,867
16		17	(a)	Bristol R	D	1-1	Shoulder	7,626
17		24	(a)	Swansea C	W	3-2	Hibbitt, Rafferty, Shoulder	15,442
18	Dec	1	(h)	Fulham	W	2-0	Rafferty, Withe	23,485
19		8	(a)	Luton T	D	1-1	Rafferty	14,845
20		15	(h)	QPR	W	4-2	Withe 2, Shoulder, Cassidy	25,027
21		22	(a)	Notts Co	D	2-2	Shoulder, Connolly	11,224
22		26	(a)	Burnley	L	2-3	Shoulder, Barton	16,433
23		29	(h)	Charlton Ath	W	2-0	Shoulder, Cassidy	26,225
24	Jan	1	(h)	Sunderland	W	3-1	Cartwright, Shoulder (pen), Cassidy	38,784
25		12	(a)	Chelsea	L	0-4		32,281
26		19	(h)	Orient	W	2-0	Connolly, Barton	20,954
27	Feb	2	(a)	Leicester C	L	0-1		24,549
28		9	(a)	Wrexham	L	0-1		13,299
29		20	(h)	Birmingham C	D	0-0		27,069
30		23	(a)	Shrewsbury T	L	1-3	Shoulder (pen)	10,833
31	Mar	1	(h)	Watford	L	0-2		23,091
32		8	(a)	Cambridge U	D	0-0		6,908
33		15	(h)	West Ham U	D	0-0		25,474
34		22	(a)	Cardiff C	D	1-1	Shinton	9,304
35		29	(h)	Bristol R	W	3-1	Withe 2, Cassidy	18,975
36	Apr	2	(h)	Notts Co	D	2-2	Shoulder, Cassidy	22,005
37		5	(a)	Sunderland	L	0-1		41,752
38		7	(h)	Burnley	D	1-1	Davies	18,863
39		12	(a)	Fulham	L	0-1		7,152
40		19	(h)	Swansea C	L	1-3	Shoulder (pen)	14,314
41		26	(a)	QPR	L	1-2	Ferguson	11,245
42	May	3	(h)	Luton T	D	2-2	Shoulder, Rafferty	13,765

FINAL LEAGUE POSITION: 9th in Division Two

Appearances

Sub. Appearances

Goals

Hardwick	Brownlie	Davies	Martin	Barton	Bird	Shoulder	Cassidy	Withe	Hibbitt	Pearson	Nicholson	Cartwright	Boam	Walker	Mitchell	Connolly	Rafferty	Carney	Cropley	Shinton	Ferguson	Wharton	Carr	No.
1	2	3	4	5	6	7	8	9	10	11														1
1	2	3	4	5	6	7	8	9	10	11														2
1	2	3	4	5	6	7	8	9	10		11*	12												3
1	2	3	4	5		7	8*	9	10		12	11	6											4
1	2	3	4	5		7	8*	9	10			11	6	12										5
1	2	3	4	5		7	8	9	10			11	6											6
1	2	3	4	5		7	8	9	10			11	6											7
1	2	3	4	5		7	8	9	10			11	6											8
1	2	3	4	5		7		9	10			11	6	8										9
1	2	3	4	5		7		9	10			11	6	8										10
1	2		4	5		7	8	9	10				6	11	3									11
1	2	3	4	5		7	8*	9	10			12	6				11							12
1	2	3	4	5		7	12	9*				11	6	8			10							13
1	2	12	4	5		7		9				11	6	8*	3		10							14
1	2	3	4	5		7		9	11				6	8			10							15
1	2	3	4	5		7		9	11*			8	6			12	10							16
1	2	3	4	5		7		9	11			8*	6			12	10							17
1			4	5		7		9	11			8	6		3		10	2						18
1	2	4*		5		7		9	11			8	6			12	10	3						19
1	2	3		5		7	4	9	11			8*	6			12	10							20
1	2	3		5		7	4	9*	11			8	6			12	10							21
1	2	3		5		7	4*		11			8	6			9	10	12						22
1	2	3		5		7	4		11			8	6			9	10							23
1	2	3		5		7	4	9	11			8	6				10							24
1	2	3		5		7	4	9	11			8	6			12	10*							25
1	2	3		5		7	4	9				8	6			11		10						26
1	2	3*		5		7	4					8	6			11	12	10						27
1	2	3				7*	4	9				8	6			11	12	5	10					28
1		3				7	4	9				8	5			11	12	2	10*					29
1	2					7		9	11			8	5			12	10	3	4*					30
1	2	3*		5		7	4	9	11			8	6				10	12						31
1	2	3			6		4	9	10			8	5	7						11				32
1	2	3			6		4		10			8	5	7			9			11				33
1	2	3			6		4	9	10			8	5	7						11				34
1	2	3			6	12	4	9	10			8	5	7*						11				35
1	2	3			6	7	4	9	10			8	5							11				36
1		3			6	7	4	9	10			8*	5	12				2		11				37
1		3			6	7	4	9*					5	8			10	2		11	12			38
1	2	3			6		4	9	10				5	7						11	8			39
1	2			5			4*	9	10			12	6	7				3		11	8			40
1	2	3			6		4	9				8	5	7			10			11*	12			41
	2	3			6		4	9	10				5	7						11	8	1		42
41	38	36	19	32	9	40	29	37	34	2	1	33	38	11	6	8	19	10	3	10	4	1	1	
		1					1	1			1	3			2			7	5	1	1			
		1		2		20	6	11	2			3					2	4		1	1			

1980-81

#	Month	Date		Opponent		Result	Scorers	Attendance
1	Aug	16	(a)	Sheffield W	L	0-2		26,164
2		20	(h)	Notts Co	D	1-1	Shoulder	17,272
3		23	(a)	Bolton W	L	0-4		11,835
4		30	(h)	Luton T	W	2-1	Koenan, Hibbitt	13,175
5	Sep	6	(h)	Cardiff C	W	2-1	Clarke, Shoulder (pen)	15,787
6		13	(a)	QPR	W	2-1	Hibbitt, Boam	10,865
7		20	(h)	Oldham Ath	D	0-0		19,786
8		27	(a)	Bristol R	D	0-0		5,171
9	Oct	4	(h)	West Ham U	D	0-0		24,866
10		7	(a)	Preston NE	W	3-2	Rafferty, Shinton 2	5,301
11		11	(a)	Bristol C	L	0-2		10,539
12		18	(h)	Swansea C	L	1-2	Rafferty	16,278
13		22	(h)	Shrewsbury T	W	1-0	Shinton	11,985
14		25	(a)	Chelsea	L	0-6		22,916
15	Nov	1	(h)	Watford	W	2-1	Hibbitt, Shinton	14,590
16		8	(a)	Cambridge U	L	1-2	Shinton	5,684
17		11	(a)	Notts Co	D	0-0		8,093
18		15	(h)	Sheffield W	W	1-0	Shinton	19,145
19		22	(h)	Wrexham	L	0-1		15,941
20		29	(a)	Orient	D	1-1	Shinton	5,800
21	Dec	13	(a)	Swansea C	L	0-4		11,672
22		20	(h)	Bristol C	D	0-0		14,131
23		26	(a)	Grimsby T	D	0-0		17,623
24		27	(h)	Derby Co	L	0-2		20,886
25	Jan	10	(a)	Wrexham	D	0-0		6,437
26		17	(a)	Luton T	W	1-0	Harford	10,774
27		31	(h)	Bolton W	W	2-1	Clarke, Martin	19,143
28	Feb	7	(h)	QPR	W	1-0	Waddle	20,404
29		21	(h)	Bristol R	D	0-0		14,364
30		25	(a)	Cardiff C	L	0-1		4,235
31		28	(a)	Oldham Ath	D	0-0		5,887
32	Mar	7	(a)	West Ham U	L	0-1		26,274
33		14	(h)	Preston NE	W	2-0	Harford 2	12,015
34		21	(a)	Shrewsbury T	L	0-1		4,975
35		28	(h)	Chelsea	W	1-0	Halliday	17,297
36	Apr	4	(a)	Watford	D	0-0		10,986
37		11	(h)	Cambridge U	W	2-1	Shoulder, (og)	11,013
38		15	(h)	Blackburn R	D	0-0		13,128
39		18	(a)	Derby Co	L	0-2		14,139
40		20	(h)	Grimsby T	D	1-1	Shoulder	13,170
41		25	(a)	Blackburn R	L	0-3		10,609
42	May	2	(h)	Orient	W	3-1	Walker, Harford, Trewick	11,639

FINAL LEAGUE POSITION: 11th in Division Two

Appearances

Sub. Appearances

Goals

Carr	Kelly	Davies	Cartwright	Boam	Carney	Rafferty	Shinton	Clarke	Wharton	Koenan	Shoulder	Barton	Hardwick	Walker	Nicholson	Hibbitt	Mitchell	Martin	Withe	Waddle	Halliday	Johnson	Trewick	Harford	Brownlie				
1	2	3	4	5	6	7	8	9	10	11																			1
1	2	3	12	5		7	8*	9	10	11	4	6																	2
1	2	3	12	5		7	8	9	10	11*	4	6																	3
		3		5	2	9			12	11	7	6*	1	4	8	10													4
		3		5	2	8		9		11	7		1	4		10	6												5
		3	12	5	2	8		9		11	7		1	4		10*	6												6
		3		5	2	8		9		11	7		1	4		10	6												7
1	2	3		5	6	8		9		11	7			4		10													8
1	2	3		5		10		9		11	7			4		8	6												9
1	2	3		5		10		9			7			4		11	6	8											10
1	2	3	12	5		10		9	8		7*					11	6	4											11
1	2	3		5		10		9	8		7					11	6	4											12
1				5	2	10	7		8							11	6	4	3	9									13
1		8		5	2	10	7		11	12								4	3	9*	6								14
1				5	2		7	9	8		10					11	6	4				3							15
1				5	2		7	9	8		10					11	6	4				3							16
1				5	2		7	9	8		10					11	6	4				3							17
1				5	2		7	9	8		10					11	6	4				3							18
1				5	2		7	9	8		10					11	6	4				3							19
1				5	2	9	7		8	11	10						6	4				3							20
1		9		5	2		7		8	11*	10				12		6	4				3							21
1				5	2		7		11		10						6	4		9		3	8						22
1				5	2		7		10								6	4		11		3	8	9					23
1				5	2		7		10							12	6*	4		11		3	8	9					24
1				5	2		7		10									4		11	6	3	8	9					25
1				5	2		7		10									4		11	6	3	8	9					26
1				5	2		7	9	10									4		11	6	3	8						27
1				5	2		7	9	10									4*		11	6	3	8	12					28
1				5	4				10		7									11	6	3	8	9	2				29
1		7	4	5					10*						12					11	6	3	8	9	2				30
1		3		5	12				10		7							4		11*	6		8	9	2				31
1		3			12				10		7	5						4		11*	6		8	9	2				32
1		3							10		7	5		11				4			6		8	9	2				33
1		3			12				10		7	5*		11				4			6		8	9	2				34
1		3			12				10		7	5		11				4*			6		8	9	2				35
1		3							10		7	5		11				4			6		8	9	2				36
1		3							10		7	5		11				4			6		8	9	2				37
1		3							10		7	5		11				4			6		8	9	2				38
1		3							10		7	5		11				4			6		8	9	2				39
1		3							10		7	5		11				4			6		8	9	2				40
1		3							10		7	5		11				4			6		8	9	2				41
1		3							10		7	5		11				4			6		8	9	2				42
38	8	25	4	31	23	15	23	14	35	11	32	14	4	17	1	15	18	31	2	13	19	16	21	18	14				
			4		4					1	1		1	1		1								1					
			1		2	7	2			1	4			1		3		1	1	1	1		1	4					

45

1981-82

1	Aug	29	(h)	Watford	L	0-1		19,244
2	Sep	5	(a)	QPR	L	0-3		14,176
3		12	(h)	Cambridge U	W	1-0	Trewick	14,666
4		19	(a)	Norwich C	L	1-2	Waddle	14,384
5		23	(h)	Shrewsbury T	W	2-0	Wharton, Shinton	13,783
6		26	(h)	Orient	W	1-0	Trewick	13,737
7		29	(a)	Bolton W	L	0-1		6,429
8	Oct	3	(a)	Cardiff C	W	4-0	Varadi 3, Davies (pen)	5,764
9		10	(h)	Derby Co	W	3-0	Wharton, Varadi 2	17,224
10		17	(a)	Barnsley	L	0-1		18,477
11		24	(h)	Rotherham U	D	1-1	Shinton	19,052
12		31	(a)	Oldham Ath	L	1-3	Davies	9,010
13	Nov	7	(a)	Chelsea	L	1-2	Waddle	16,509
14		14	(h)	Charlton Ath	W	4-1	Wharton, Varadi 2, Brown	15,254
15		21	(h)	Luton T	W	3-2	Varadi, Brown 2	21,084
16		24	(a)	Orient	L	0-1		4,026
17		28	(a)	Grimsby T	D	1-1	Wharton	9,256
18	Dec	5	(h)	Blackburn R	D	0-0		18,775
19	Jan	16	(a)	Watford	W	3-2	Varadi, Todd 2	12,333
20		30	(h)	Norwich C	W	2-1	Varadi, Mills	14,492
21	Feb	3	(h)	Bolton W	W	2-0	Wharton, Trewick (pen)	14,714
22		6	(a)	Cambridge U	L	0-1		5,092
23		13	(h)	Cardiff C	W	2-1	Varadi, Trewick	15,129
24		20	(a)	Shrewsbury T	D	0-0		4,636
25		24	(h)	Sheffield W	W	1-0	Varadi	19,174
26		27	(a)	Derby Co	D	2-2	Waddle, Varadi	12,257
27	Mar	3	(a)	Leicester C	L	0-3		12,497
28		6	(h)	Barnsley	W	1-0	Varadi	18,784
29		13	(a)	Rotherham U	D	0-0		16,905
30		20	(h)	Oldham Ath	W	2-0	Mills, Brownlie	18,531
31		27	(h)	Chelsea	W	1-0	Waddle	26,994
32		31	(h)	Crystal Palace	D	0-0		22,151
33	Apr	3	(a)	Charlton Ath	W	1-0	Waddle	6,357
34		6	(a)	Wrexham	L	2-4	Varadi 2	4,517
35		10	(h)	Leicester C	D	0-0		25,777
36		12	(a)	Sheffield W	L	1-2	Barton	29,917
37		17	(a)	Luton T	L	2-3	Mills, Trewick (pen)	13,041
38		24	(h)	Grimsby T	L	0-1		14,065
39	May	1	(a)	Blackburn R	L	1-4	Varadi	5,207
40		5	(h)	QPR	L	0-4		10,748
41		8	(h)	Wrexham	W	4-2	Waddle, Varadi, Trewick (pen), Brownlie	9,419
42		15	(a)	Crystal Palace	W	2-1	Waddle, Mills (pen)	8,453

FINAL LEAGUE POSITION: 9th in Division Two

Appearances

Sub. Appearances

Goals

Carr	Brownlie	Davies	Trewick	Barton	Halliday	Walker	Shoulder	Varadi	Wharton	Waddle	Martin	Haddock	Carney	Shinton	Todd	Saunders	Brown	Pugh	Mills	Cartwright	Bell	Ferris	
1	2	3	4	5	6*	7	8	9	10	11	12												1
1		3	4	5	6	7	8	9	10*	11	12	2											2
1	2	3	4	5	6	7		9	10	11	8												3
1	2	3	4	5*	6	7		9	10	11	8		12										4
1	2	3	4	5	6	12		9*	10	11	8			7									5
1	2	3	4	5	6			9	10	11	8			7									6
1	2	3	4	5	6			9	10	11	8			7									7
1	2	3	4	5	6			9	10*	11	8	12		7									8
1	2	3	4	5	6			9	10	11*	8			7	12								9
1	2	3	4	5	6			9	10	11	8			7									10
1	2	3	4	5	6	12		9	10*	11	8			7									11
1	2	3*	4	5				9	10	11	8	12	6	7									12
1	2		4					9*	10	11	8	6	5			3	7	12					13
1	2		4					9	10	11	8	6	5			3	7						14
1	2		4			12		9	10	11	8	6	5			3	7*						15
1	2		4			7		9	10	11	8	6	5			3							16
1	2		4					9	10	11	8	6	5			3	7						17
1	2		4			12		9	10	11	8	6	5			3	7*						18
1	2		4					9	10	11	8	6	5		7	3							19
1	2		4					9	10	11	8	6	5			3			7				20
1			4	5				9	10	11	8	6	2			3			7				21
1			4*	5				9	10	11	8	6	2		12	3			7				22
1	2		4	5				9	10	11	8	6				3			7				23
1	2		4					9	10	11	8*	6	5			3			7	12			24
1	2		4					9	10	11		6	5			3			7	8			25
1	2		4					9	10	11		6	5			3			7	8			26
1	2		4					9	10	11		6	5			3			7	8			27
1	2		4			12		9		11	8	6	5			3			7*	10			28
1	2		4					9		11	8	6	5			3			7	10			29
1	2		4			12		9		11	8	6*	5			3			7	10			30
1	2		4					9		11	8	6	5			3			7	10			31
1	2		4					9		11	8	6	5			3			7	10			32
1	2		4					9		11	8	6	5			3			7	10			33
1	2		4*					9	12	11	8	6	5			3			7	10			34
1	2		4	5		12		9		11	8*	6				3			7	10			35
1	2		4	5				9		11	8	6				3			7	10			36
1	2		4	5*				9	12	11	8	6				3			7	10			37
1	2		4					9	12	11	8	6	5			3*			7	10			38
1	2	3						9	10	11*	8	6	5						7		4	12	39
1	2		4*					9		11	8	6	5			3			7		10	12	40
1	2		4	5	6			9	12	11	8					3			7	10			41
1			4*	5	6			9	12	11	8		2			3			7	10			42
42	38	13	40	20	13	5	3	42	28	42	37	28	27	8	1	29	5		23	16	2		
						7			5		2	2	1	1				1		1		2	
		2	2	6	1			18	5	7			2	2			3		4				

1982-83

1	Aug	28	(h)	QPR	W	1-0	Keegan	35,718
2	Sep	1	(a)	Blackburn R	W	2-1	Keegan, Martin	14,421
3		4	(a)	Bolton W	L	1-3	Keegan (pen)	17,707
4		8	(h)	Middlesbrough	D	1-1	Channon	27,984
5		11	(h)	Chelsea	D	1-1	Clarke	29,136
6		18	(a)	Shrewsbury T	L	1-2	Varadi	7,907
7		25	(h)	Barnsley	L	1-2	Varadi	24,522
8	Oct	2	(a)	Rotherham U	W	5-1	Todd, Keegan 4 (1 pen)	12,436
9		9	(a)	Oldham Ath	D	2-2	Varadi 2	9,000
10		16	(h)	Fulham	L	1-4	Keegan (pen)	29,647
11		23	(h)	Crystal Palace	W	1-0	Waddle	22,616
12		30	(a)	Leeds U	L	1-3	Anderson	26,570
13	Nov	6	(h)	Burnley	W	3-0	Waddle, Varadi, Keegan	20,961
14		13	(a)	Leicester C	D	2-2	Keegan 2	15,044
15		20	(a)	Carlisle U	L	0-2		16,276
16		27	(h)	Cambridge U	W	2-0	McDermott, Martin	20,385
17	Dec	4	(a)	Charlton Ath	L	0-2		10,381
18		11	(h)	Wolverhampton W	D	1-1	Wharton	19,595
19		18	(a)	Sheffield W	D	1-1	Varadi	16,310
20		27	(h)	Derby Co	W	1-0	Gayle	30,558
21		28	(a)	Grimsby T	D	2-2	Varadi, Gayle	14,983
22	Jan	1	(h)	Carlisle U	D	2-2	Keegan 2	28,578
23		3	(h)	Bolton W	D	2-2	Waddle, Martin	23,533
24		15	(a)	QPR	L	0-2		13,972
25		22	(h)	Shrewsbury R	W	4-0	Wharton 2, Varadi, Keegan (pen)	19,333
26	Feb	5	(a)	Middlesbrough	D	1-1	Keegan	25,184
27		19	(h)	Oldham Ath	W	1-0	McDermott	20,689
28		26	(a)	Fulham	D	2-2	McDermott, Varadi	14,277
29	Mar	5	(a)	Crystal Palace	W	2-0	Waddle, Varadi	10,239
30		12	(h)	Leeds U	W	2-1	Waddle, Keegan (pen)	24,543
31		19	(a)	Burnley	L	0-1		13,900
32		26	(h)	Leicester C	D	2-2	McDermott, Keegan	22,692
33	Apr	2	(h)	Grimsby T	W	4-0	Varadi 2, McDonald, Keegan	20,202
34		4	(a)	Derby Co	L	1-2	Waddle	19,779
35		9	(h)	Blackburn R	W	3-2	Waddle, Varadi, (og)	17,839
36		16	(a)	Chelsea	W	2-0	Varadi, Keegan (pen)	13,446
37		20	(h)	Rotherham U	W	4-0	McDermott, Varadi, Keegan, Wharton	18,523
38		23	(h)	Charlton Ath	W	4-2	McDermott, Varadi 2, Wharton	20,567
39		30	(a)	Cambridge U	L	0-1		7,591
40	May	4	(a)	Barnsley	W	5-0	Varadi 2, McDonald 2, Keegan	10,958
41		7	(h)	Sheffield W	W	2-1	Varadi, (og)	29,874
42		14	(a)	Wolverhampton W	D	2-2	Varadi, McDonald	22,446

FINAL LEAGUE POSITION: 5th in Division Two

Appearances

Sub. Appearances

Goals

48

Hardwick	Craggs	Saunders	Trewick	Clarke	Haddock	Keegan	Martin	Varadi	Cartwright	Waddle	Wharton	Anderson	Channon	Bell	McDonald	Todd	Carr	Carney	McDermott	McCreery	Hedworth	Gayle	Ferris	Thomas	
1	2	3	4*	5	6	7	8	9	10	11	12														1
1	2	3		5	6	7	4	9	8	11*	10	12													2
1	2	3		5	6	7	4	9	8	11	10														3
1	2	3		5	6	7	4	9	10	11			8												4
1	2	3		5	6	7	4	9		11*	10		8	12											5
1	2	3		5	6	7	4	9			10	12	8	11*											6
1	2	3		5	6	7	4*	9			10		8		11	12									7
		3		5		7	4	9		11		2				8	1	6	10						8
		3		5		7	4	9		12		2				8*	1	6	10	11					9
		3		5		7	4	9		12		2				8*	1	6	10	11					10
		3		5	6	7	4	9		11	10	2					1			8					11
					6	7	4	9*		11	3	2					1	5	10	8	12				12
					6	7	4*	9		11	3	2			12		1	5	10	8					13
					6	7	4	9		11	3	2					1	5	10	8					14
	12			5			4	9		11	3	2				7*	1	6	10	8					15
	12			5			4	9*		11	3	2					1		10	8	6	7			16
				5			4			11	3	2					1	12	10	8	6	9	7*		17
				5			4	9			3	2			11		1		10	8	6	7			18
				5	6			9		11	3	2*			4		1	12	10	8		7			19
	2			5	6	7		9		11	3						1		10	4		8			20
				5	6	7	12	9		11	3						1	2	10	4*		8			21
	2			5	6	7	12	9		11	3						1		10	4*		8			22
				5	6	7	4	9			3	2			12		1		10	11*		8			23
				5		7	4	9*		11	3	2			8		1	6	10				12		24
		3		5		7*	4	9		11	10	2			8		1	6					12		25
		3		5		7	4	9		11	10	2			8		1	6							26
				5		7	4	9		11*	3	2			8		1	6	10				12		27
				5		7	4	9		11	3	2			8		1	6	10						28
				5		7	4	9		11	3	2			8		1	6	10						29
				5		7	4	9		11	3	2			8		1	6	10						30
				5		7	4	9		11	3	2			8		1	6	10						31
				5		7	4	9		11	3	2			8*		1	6	10	12					32
				5		7	4	9		11	3	2			8		1	6	10*	12					33
				5		7	4*	9		11	3	2			8		1	6	10	12					34
				5		7		9*		11	3	2			8		1	6	10	4			12		35
				5		7		9		11	3	2			8		1	6	10	4					36
				5		7	12	9		11*	3	2			8		1	6	10	4					37
				5		7	12	9		11	3	2*			8		1	6	10	4					38
	2			5		7	12	9		11	3				8*		1	6	10	4					39
				5		7		9		11	3	2			8			6	10	4				1	40
				5		7		9		11	3	2			8			6	10	4				1	41
				5		7	12	9		11	3	2			8*			6	10	4				1	42
7	10	13	1	39	17	37	29	39	4	37	38	31	4	1	22	4	32	27	32	23	3	8	1	3	
	2						6				3	2		1	2	1		2		3	1		4		
				1		21	3	21		7	5	1	1		4	1			6			2			

1983-84

1	Aug	27	(a)	Leeds U	W	1-0	Anderson	30,806
2		29	(h)	Shrewsbury T	L	0-1		29,123
3	Sep	3	(h)	Oldham A	W	3-0	McDermott, Waddle, Mills	22,644
4		6	(a)	Middlesbrough	L	2-3	Keegan, Mills	19,648
5		10	(a)	Grimsby T	D	1-1	Keegan	9,000
6		17	(h)	Crystal Palace	W	3-1	Ryan, Waddle, Keegan	22,774
7		24	(a)	Barnsley	D	1-1	Waddle	14,085
8	Oct	1	(h)	Portsmouth	W	4-2	Waddle 2, Keegan (pen), Wharton	25,411
9		8	(h)	Charlton A	W	2-1	Keegan 2	23,247
10		16	(a)	Swansea C	W	2-1	Wharton, Mills	9,807
11		19	(a)	Cardiff C	W	2-0	Keegan, Beardsley	9,926
12		29	(h)	Manchester C	W	5-0	Beardsley 3, Keegan, Waddle	33,588
13	Nov	5	(h)	Fulham	W	3-2	Keegan, Mills, Wharton	31,568
14		12	(a)	Chelsea	L	0-4		30,628
15		19	(a)	Sheffield W	L	2-4	McDermott, Keegan (pen)	41,134
16		26	(h)	Cambridge U	W	2-1	Keegan (pen), Beardsley	25,005
17	Dec	3	(a)	Derby Co	L	2-3	Keegan, Waddle	18,691
18		10	(h)	Huddersfield T	W	5-2	Keegan, Beardsley, Waddle 2, McDermott	25,652
19		17	(a)	Brighton & HA	W	1-0	Waddle	13,896
20		26	(h)	Blackburn R	D	1-1	Waddle	33,802
21		27	(a)	Carlisle U	L	1-3	Waddle	14,756
22		31	(a)	Oldham A	W	2-1	Keegan 2	8,518
23	Jan	2	(h)	Barnsley	W	1-0	Waddle	29,833
24		21	(a)	Crystal Palace	L	1-3	Beardsley	9,464
25	Feb	4	(a)	Portsmouth	W	4-1	Keegan 2, Beardsley 2	18,686
26		11	(h)	Grimsby T	L	0-1		28,526
27		18	(a)	Manchester C	W	2-1	Beardsley, Keegan	41,767
28		25	(h)	Cardiff C	W	3-1	Waddle, Keegan 2 (1 pen)	27,909
29	Mar	3	(a)	Fulham	D	2-2	Beardsley, Keegan	12,290
30		10	(h)	Chelsea	D	1-1	McDermott	36,506
31		17	(h)	Middlesbrough	W	3-1	Beardsley, McDermott, Keegan	30,386
32		24	(a)	Shrewsbury T	D	2-2	Johnson (og), Keegan	8,313
33		28	(h)	Leeds U	W	1-0	Irwin (og)	30,877
34		31	(h)	Swansea C	W	2-0	Wharton, Beardsley	27,308
35	Apr	7	(a)	Charlton A	W	3-1	Waddle, McDermott, Beardsley	15,289
36		14	(h)	Sheffield W	L	0-1		36,725
37		20	(a)	Blackburn R	D	1-1	Trewick	19,196
38		23	(h)	Carlisle U	W	5-1	Keegan 2, Waddle, Beardsley 2	33,386
39		28	(a)	Cambridge U	L	0-1		7,720
40	May	5	(h)	Derby Co	W	4-0	Keegan, Beardsley 2, Waddle	35,850
41		7	(a)	Huddersfield T	D	2-2	Beardsley, Mills	25,101
42		12	(h)	Brighton & HA	W	3-1	Keegan, Waddle, Beardsley	36,415

FINAL LEAGUE POSITION: 3rd in Division Two

Appearances

Sub Appearances

Goals

50

Carr	Anderson	Ryan	McCreery	Clarke	Carney	Keegan	McDonald	Mills	McDermott	Waddle	Wharton	Thomas	Trewick	Beardsley	Saunders	Haddock	Roeder	
1*	2	3	4	5	6	7	8	9	10	11	12							1
	2	3	4	5	6	7	8*	9	10	11	12	1						2
	2	3	4	5	6	7	8	9	10	11		1						3
	2	3	4	5	6	7	8*	9	10	11	12	1						4
	2	3	4	5	6	7		9	10	11	8	1						5
	2	3	4	5	6	7		9	10	11	8*	1	12					6
	2	3	4	5*	6	7		9	10	11	8	1		12				7
	2	3	4		6	7		12	10	9*	11	1		8	5			8
	2	3	4		6	7		12	10	9	11*	1		8	5			9
	2	3	4		6	7		12	10	11*	8	1		9	5			10
	2	3	4		6	7			10	9	11	1		8	5			11
	2	3	4		6	7			10	9	11	1		8	5			12
	2	3	4		6	7		12	10	9	11	1		8	5			13
	2	3	4*		6	7		12	10	9	11	1		8	5			14
	2	3			6	7		4	10	9	11	1		8	5			15
	2	3			6	7		4	10	9	11	1		8	5			16
		3	4*		6	7		12	10	9	11	1		8	5	2		17
	2	3*	4		6	7		12	10	9	11	1		8	5			18
	2		4		6	7		11	10	9	3	1		8	5			19
	2		4			7	12	11*	10	9	3	1		8	5		6	20
	2		4		11	7			10	9	3	1		8	5		6	21
	2	3	4			7	8		10	9*	11	1	12		5		6	22
	2	3	4			7			10	9	11	1		8	5		6	23
1	2	3	4	5		7			10	9	11			8			6	24
1	2	11*	4	5	12	7			10	9	3			8			6	25
1	2		4	5		7	11		10	9	3			8			6	26
1	2		4	5		7			10	9	3		11	8			6	27
1	2		4	5		7			10	9	3		11	8			6	28
	2		4	5		7			10	9	3	1	11	8			6	29
1	2		4	5		7			10	9	3		11	8			6	30
1	2		4		5	7			10	9	3		11	8			6	31
1	2		4		5	7			10	9	3		11	8			6	32
1	2		4		5	7			10	9	3		11	8			6	33
1	2		4		5	7			10	9	3		11	8			6	34
1	2		4		5	7			10	9	3		11	8			6	35
1	2		4		5	7			10	9	3		11	8			6	36
1	2		4		5	7			10	9	3		11*	8		12	6	37
1	2		4		5	7	11		10	9	3			8			6	38
1	2		4		5	7	11*		10	9	3			8		12	6	39
1	2		4		5	7			10	9	3		11	8			6	40
1	2		4		5		8		10	9	3		11	7			6	41
1	2		4		5	7			10	9	3		11	8			6	42
19	41	22	40	14	32	41	10	10	42	42	38	23	14	34	16	1	23	
				1			2	6			3		2	1		2		
	1	1				27	5		6	18	4		1	20				

1984-85

1	Aug	25	(a)	Leicester C	W	3-2	Carney, McCreery, Waddle	18,636
2		27	(h)	Sheffield W	W	2-1	Beardsley (pen), Wharton	29,700
3	Sep	1	(h)	Aston Villa	W	3-0	Beardsley, Waddle 2	31,497
4		4	(a)	Arsenal	L	0-2		37,078
5		8	(a)	Manchester U	L	0-5		54,915
6		15	(h)	Everton	L	2-3	Beardsley (pen), Wharton	26,944
7		22	(a)	QPR	D	5-5	McDonald, Waddle 3, Wharton	14,144
8		29	(h)	West Ham U	D	1-1	Beardsley	29,452
9	Oct	6	(h)	Ipswich T	W	3-0	Burley (og), Heard, Waddle	25,094
10		13	(a)	Coventry C	D	1-1	Beardsley (pen)	14,091
11		20	(h)	Nottingham F	D	1-1	Wharton	28,252
12		27	(a)	Watford	D	3-3	Beardsley, McDonald, Wharton	18,753
13	Nov	3	(a)	Luton T	D	2-2	Beardsley, Heard	10,009
14		10	(h)	Chelsea	W	2-1	McDonald, Waddle	23,723
15		18	(h)	Liverpool	L	0-2		28,003
16		24	(a)	Southampton	L	0-1		18,895
17	Dec	1	(h)	Stoke C	W	2-1	Anderson (pen), Waddle	21,135
18		8	(a)	Tottenham H	L	1-3	Waddle	29,695
19		15	(h)	Norwich C	D	1-1	Waddle	20,030
20		22	(a)	Aston Villa	L	0-4		14,491
21		26	(a)	West Brom A	L	1-2	Baird	20,405
22		29	(h)	Arsenal	L	1-3	Beardsley (pen)	27,349
23	Jan	1	(h)	Sunderland	W	3-1	Beardsley 3 (1 pen)	36,821
24		12	(a)	Everton	L	0-4		32,156
25	Feb	2	(a)	West Ham U	D	1-1	Waddle	17,723
26		9	(h)	Manchester U	D	1-1	Beardsley	31,798
27		16	(a)	Chelsea	L	0-1		21,826
28		23	(h)	Luton T	W	1-0	Wharton	23,737
29	Mar	2	(h)	Watford	W	3-1	Cunningham, Megson, Reilly	24,923
30		9	(a)	Nottingham F	D	0-0		17,425
31		20	(h)	Leicester C	L	1-4	Beardsley	21,967
32		23	(a)	Ipswich T	D	1-1	McDonald	14,366
33		30	(a)	Sheffield W	L	2-4	Beardsley (pen), Waddle	26,525
34	Apr	6	(h)	West Brom A	W	1-0	Beardsley	22,690
35		8	(a)	Sunderland	D	0-0		28,246
36		13	(h)	QPR	W	1-0	Reilly	21,711
37		17	(h)	Coventry C	L	0-1		19,578
38		20	(a)	Liverpool	L	1-3	McDonald	34,733
39		27	(h)	Southampton	W	2-1	Reilly, Wharton	20,871
40	May	4	(a)	Stoke C	W	1-0	Dyson (og)	7,088
41		6	(h)	Tottenham H	L	2-3	Beardsley 2 (2 pens)	29,702
42		11	(a)	Norwich C	D	0-0		18,399

FINAL LEAGUE POSITION: 14th in Division One   Appearances

Sub Appearances

Goals

Carr	Brown	Ryan	Carney	Roeder	Saunders	McDonald	Wharton	Waddle	Beardsley	McCreery	Anderson	Ferris	Haddock	Heard	Hedworth	Clarke	Megson	Allon	Baird	Thomas	Cunningham	Reilly	Gascoigne	
1	2	3	4	5	6	7	8	9	10	11														1
1	2	3	4	5	6	7	8	9	10	11*	12													2
1	2	3	4	5	6	7	8	9	10	11														3
1	2	3	4	5	6	7	8	9	10	11														4
1	2	3*	4	5	6	7	8	9	10	11	12													5
1	2	3	4*	5	6	7	8	9	10	11		12												6
1	2			6	3	7	8	9	10	11	5		4											7
1	2			6	3	7	8	9	10	11	5			4										8
1	2			6	3	7	8	9	10	11	5			4										9
1	2			6	3	7	8	9	10	11	5			4										10
1	2				3	7	8	9	10	11	5	12		4	6*									11
1	2				3	7	8	9	10	11	5			4		6								12
1	2				3	7	8	9	10	11	5			4		6								13
1	2				3	7	8	9*	10	11	5	12		4		6								14
1	2			6	3	7*	8	9	10	11	5	12		4										15
1	2			6	3	7	8	9	10*	11	5			4			12							16
1	2			6	3	12	8	9		11	5			4			7	10*						17
1	2			6	3	12	8	9	10	11	5			4*			7							18
1	2			6	3		8	9	10	11	5			4			7							19
1	2					8	11	9	4		5			3		6	7		10					20
1	2		4			11	8	9			5			3		6	7		10					21
1	2			6			8	9	10	11*	5			3		4	7		12					22
1	2				3	11	8		10		5			4		6	7		9					23
1	2		4		3	12	8	9		11	5*					6	7		10					24
	2			5		7	3	9	10	11				4		6	8			1				25
	2			6		4	3	9	10	11	5					7				1	8			26
	2			5		4	3	9		11*	12			10		6	7			1	8			27
	2			6		3		9	10	11	5			4						1	8	7		28
	2			6			3	9	10	11	5			4						1	8	7		29
	2			6			3	9	10	11	5			4						1	8	7		30
	2			6		12	3	9	10	11	5			4*						1	8	7		31
	2			6		7	3	12	10	11	5			4						1	8	9*		32
	2			6		12	3	9*	10	11	5			4						1	8	7		33
	2			6		12	3		10	11	5			4		7*				1	8	9		34
	2			6		7	3		10	11	5			4						1	8	9		35
	2			6		7	3		10	11	5			4						1	8	9*	12	36
	2			6		12	3		10	11	5			4		7				1	8*	9		37
	2			6		12	3	9	10	11	5			4		7*				1	8			38
	2*			6		7	3	9	10	11	12			4		5				1	8			39
				6		7	3	9	10	11	2			4		5				1	8			40
				6		7	3	9	10	11	2			4*		5				1	8	12		41
				6		7	3	9	10	11	2			4		5				1	8			42
24	39	6	6	36	21	29	35	35	38	34	31		1	34	1	23	19	1	4	18	13	14		
						7		1		1	4	4		1		1		1				2		
		1				5	7	13	17	1	1			2		1		1		1	3			

1985-86

1	Aug	17	(a)	Southampton	D	1-1	Beardsley (pen)	16,401
2		21	(h)	Luton T	D	2-2	Beardsley, Roeder	21,304
3		24	(h)	Liverpool	W	1-0	Reilly	29,670
4		26	(a)	Coventry C	W	2-1	Reilly, Stewart	12,097
5		31	(h)	QPR	W	3-1	McDonald, Reilly, Beardsley	25,026
6	Sep	4	(a)	Manchester U	L	0-3		51,102
7		7	(a)	Tottenham H	L	1-5	Davies	23,883
8		14	(h)	WBA	W	4-1	McDonald, Clarke, Reilly 2	21,855
9		21	(h)	Oxford U	W	3-0	Beardsley, McDonald, Gascoigne	23,596
10		28	(a)	Arsenal	D	0-0		24,104
11	Oct	5	(h)	West Ham U	L	1-2	Reilly	26,709
12		12	(a)	Ipswich T	D	2-2	Beardsley, McDonald	12,536
13		19	(h)	Nottingham F	L	0-3		23,151
14		26	(a)	Aston Villa	W	2-1	Gascoigne, Beardsley	12,633
15	Nov	2	(h)	Watford	D	1-1	Gascoigne	20,649
16		9	(a)	Birmingham C	W	1-0	Reilly	8,162
17		16	(h)	Chelsea	L	1-3	Roeder	22,355
18		23	(a)	Manchester C	L	0-1		25,179
19		30	(h)	Leicester C	W	2-1	Clarke, Beardsley	17,304
20	Dec	7	(a)	Luton T	L	0-2		10,319
21		14	(h)	Southampton	W	2-1	Roeder, Beardsley	19,229
22		21	(a)	Liverpool	D	1-1	Beardsley	30,746
23		26	(a)	Sheffield W	D	2-2	Roeder, Beardsley	30,269
24	Jan	1	(h)	Everton	D	2-2	Gascoigne, Beardsley	27,820
25		11	(a)	West Brom A	D	1-1	Wharton	9,100
26		18	(a)	QPR	L	1-3	Gascoigne	13,159
27	Feb	1	(h)	Coventry C	W	3-2	Beardsley, Allon, Wharton	16,637
28		8	(a)	Nottingham F	W	2-1	Beardsley 2	15,388
29	Mar	1	(h)	Arsenal	W	1-0	Roeder	21,860
30		15	(h)	Ipswich T	W	3-1	Beardsley, Whitehurst, Gascoigne	18,851
31		19	(a)	Oxford U	W	2-1	Gascoigne, Beardsley	10,052
32		22	(h)	Tottenham H	D	2-2	Whitehurst, Anderson	30,615
33		29	(a)	Everton	L	0-1		41,116
34		31	(h)	Sheffield W	W	4-1	Stephenson, Gascoigne, Beardsley, Whitehurst	25,614
35	Apr	5	(a)	Watford	L	1-4	McClelland (og)	14,706
36		9	(h)	Aston Villa	D	2-2	Whitehurst, Gascoigne	20,107
37		12	(h)	Birmingham C	W	4-1	Beardsley 2, Anderson, Whitehurst	19,981
38		16	(h)	Manchester U	L	2-4	Stewart, Cunningham	31,840
39		19	(a)	Chelsea	D	1-1	Anderson	18,970
40		21	(a)	West Ham U	L	1-8	Whitehurst	24,735
41		26	(h)	Manchester C	W	3-1	Clarke, Roeder, Whitehurst	22,689
42	May	3	(a)	Leicester C	L	0-2		13,171

FINAL LEAGUE POSITION: 11th in Division One

Appearances

Sub Appearances

Goals

54

Thomas	Anderson	Wharton	Davies	Clarke	Roeder	McDonald	Megson	Reilly	Beardsley	Gascoigne	McCreery	Stewart	McKinnon	Hedworth	Haddock	Cunningham	Bailey	Allon	Whitehurst	Stephenson	McKellar	#
1	2	3	4	5	6	7	8	9	10	11*	12											1
1	2	3		5	6	7	8*	9	10	4	12	11										2
1	2	3		5	6	7		9	10	4	8	11										3
1	2	3		5	6	7		9	10	4	8	11										4
1	2	3		5	6	7	12	9	10	4	8	11*										5
1	2	3		5	6	7		9	10	4	8	11										6
1	2		4	5	6	7		9	10	12	8	11	3*									7
1	3		4	5	6	7		9	10	12	8*	11		2								8
1	3		4	5	6	7		9	10	12	8	11	2*									9
1	3		4	5	6	7			10		8	11		2		9						10
1	3		4	5	6	7		9	10		8	11		2								11
1	3		4	5	6	7		9	10		8	11		2								12
1	3		4	5	6	7		9	10		8	11		2*		12						13
1	2			5	6	7	12	9*	10	8	4	11					3					14
1	2			5	6	7*		9	10	11	4	12				8	3					15
1	3	2		5	6	12		9	10	7	4	11*						8				16
1	2	11		5	6			9	10	7	4*	12					3	8				17
1	2	11	7	5	6	12		9	10	8*	4						3					18
1	4	8	2	5	6	7			10			11				9	3					19
1	7	8	2	5	6				10		4	11					3	9				20
1	2	11	8	5	6				10		4						3	9	7			21
1	2			5	6				10	8	4	11					3	9	7			22
1	2			5	6				10	8	4	11					3	9	7			23
1	2			5	6				10	8	4	11					3	9	7			24
1	2	11		5	6				10	8	4						3	9	7			25
1	2	11		5	6	12			10	8	4						3	9	7*			26
1	2	11		5	6	12			10	8*	4						3	9	7			27
1	2*	11		5	6	12			10	8	4					9	3		7			28
1	2	11		5	6				10*	8	4					12	3	9	7			29
	2			5	6	11*			10	8	4					12	3	9	7		1	30
	2			5	6				10	8	4					11	3	9	7		1	31
	2			5	6				10	8	4					11	3	9	7		1	32
	2			5	6				10	8	4	11					3	9	7		1	33
	2			5	6				10	8	4	11*				12	3	9	7		1	34
	2			5	6				10	8	4	11*				12	3	9	7		1	35
				5	6				10	8	4	11*		2		12	3	9	7		1	36
1	2			5	6	11			10	8	4						3	9	7			37
1				5	6	2			10	8*	4	11				12	3	9	7			38
	8			5	6	2			10		4					11	3	9	7		1	39
1*	5				6	2			10		4	12		8		11	3	9	7			40
				5	6	2			10		4				8	11	3	9	7		1	41
				5	6	2			10		4	11			8	9	3		7		1	42
32	38	15	14	41	42	23	2	17	42	28	39	25	1	4	6	10	28	3	20	22	10	
						5	2			3	2	3				7						
	3	2	1	3	6	4		7	19	9		2				1		1	7	1		

1986-87

1	Aug	23	(h)	Liverpool	L	0-2		33,306
2		25	(a)	Tottenham H	D	1-1	Beardsley	25,381
3		30	(a)	Luton T	D	0-0		9,254
4	Sep	3	(h)	QPR	L	0-2		23,080
5		6	(h)	Sheffield W	L	2-3	Allon, Scott	22,010
6		13	(a)	Coventry C	L	0-3		11,370
7		20	(h)	Wimbledon	W	1-0	Gascoigne	21,545
8		27	(a)	Norwich C	L	0-2		15,735
9	Oct	4	(a)	Southampton	L	1-4	Thomas A.	14,622
10		11	(h)	Manchester C	W	3-1	McDonald (pen), Gascoigne, Cunningham	21,780
11		18	(h)	Arsenal	L	1-2	Stewart	22,368
12		25	(a)	Aston Villa	L	0-2		14,614
13	Nov	1	(h)	Oxford U	D	0-0		19,622
14		8	(a)	Leicester C	D	1-1	McDonald (pen)	9,836
15		15	(h)	Watford	D	2-2	Anderson, McDonald (pen)	23,645
16		22	(a)	Chelsea	W	3-1	Thomas A. 2, Beardsley	14,544
17		30	(h)	West Ham U	W	4-0	McDonald, Thomas A. 2, Jackson D.	22,077
18	Dec	6	(a)	Charlton A	D	1-1	Goddard	7,333
19		13	(h)	Nottingham F	W	3-2	Wharton, Thomas A., Beardsley	26,191
20		21	(a)	Sheffield W	L	0-2		28,897
21		26	(h)	Everton	L	0-4		35,079
22		27	(a)	Watford	L	0-1		18,011
23	Jan	1	(a)	Manchester U	L	1-4	Jackson D.	43,334
24		3	(h)	Coventry C	L	1-2	McDonald	22,366
25		24	(a)	Liverpool	L	0-2		38,054
26	Feb	7	(h)	Luton T	D	2-2	Jackson P., Goddard	22,437
27		14	(a)	QPR	L	1-2	Goddard	10,731
28		28	(a)	Wimbledon	L	1-3	Beardsley	6,779
29	Mar	7	(h)	Aston Villa	W	2-1	Cunningham, Beardsley	21,224
30		21	(a)	Manchester C	D	0-0		23,060
31		25	(h)	Tottenham H	D	1-1	Goddard	30,782
32		28	(h)	Southampton	W	2-0	Goddard, Gascoigne	22,717
33	Apr	4	(h)	Leicester C	W	2-0	Wharton, Goddard	23,360
34		8	(h)	Norwich C	W	4-1	Goddard, Gascoigne, McDonald (pen), Jackson D.	24,534
35		11	(a)	Oxford U	D	1-1	Goddard	10,526
36		14	(a)	Arsenal	W	1-0	Goddard	17,353
37		18	(h)	Manchester U	W	2-1	Roeder, Goddard	32,706
38		20	(a)	Everton	L	0-3		43,576
39		25	(h)	Chelsea	W	1-0	Goddard	21,962
40	May	2	(a)	West Ham U	D	1-1	McDonald (pen)	17,844
41		4	(h)	Charlton A	L	0-3		26,950
42		9	(a)	Nottingham F	L	1-2	Gascoigne	17,788

FINAL LEAGUE POSITION: 17th in Division One

Appearances

Sub Appearances

Goals

Thomas M.	Anderson	Bailey	McCreery	Clarke	Roeder	Davies	Gascoigne	Whitehurst	Beardsley	Wharton	McDonald	Bogie	Allon	Stewart	Scott	Cunningham	Thomas A.	Kelly	Stephenson	Jackson D.	Jackson P.	Goddard	Nesbit	Wrightson	Craig	Tinnion	
1	2	3	4	5	6	7	8*	9	10	11	12																1
1	2	3	4	5	6	7		9	10	11	8																2
1	2	3	4		6		8	9	10	11	5	7															3
1	2	3	4		6	7	8	9		11*	5		10	12													4
1	2	3	4			7	8	9			5		10	11	6												5
1	6	3	4	5		7	8	9			2			11		10											6
	2	3	4	5	6		8	9			7			11			10	1									7
1	2*	3	4	5	6		12		10		11		9				8		7								8
1	6		4*	5		12	11	10	3	2			9				8		7								9
	6		4		5		8		10	3	2			11		9		1	7								10
	6		4		5		8		10	3	2			11*		9	4	1	7	12							11
1	3		4		6		12		10		2			11		9	8		7*		5						12
1	3		4		6		7*		10	12	2			11		9	8				5						13
1	2		4		6				10	3	7			11*			12	8			5	9					14
1	2		4		6				10	3	7						12	8*	11		5	9					15
1	2*		4		6				10	3	7						8	11		12	5	9					16
1	2		4		6				10	3	7						8	11		12	5	9*					17
1	2*		4		6				10	3	7						8	11			5	9	12				18
1			4		6				10	3	2						8	7		11*	5	9	12				19
1			4		6				10	3	2						8	7		11	5	9		4			20
1			4		6				10	3	2					12	8	7*		11	5	9		4			21
1			4		6				10	3	2						8	7		11	5	9		4			22
1			4		6				10	3	2					12	8	7*		11	5	9					23
1	4				6	2*				3	7					12	8			10	5	9			11		24
1	4				6				10	3	2					11	8	7			5	9					25
1			4*		6				10	3	2						8	7		12	5	9			11		26
1					6				10	3	2				4		8	7			5	9			11		27
1				6					10	3	2				4		8	7*			5	9			12	11	28
1	6		4						10	3	2	8*				9		7		12	5				11		29
1	11		4		6				10	3	2					9		7		12	5	8*					30
1	11		4		6		8		10	3	2					12		7			5	9					31
1	11		4		6		8		10	3	2							7			5	9					32
1	11		4		6		8		10	3	2							7			5	9					33
1	11		4*		6		8		10	3	2							7		12	5	9					34
1	11				6		8		10	3	2					12		7*		4	5	9					35
1	11				6		8		10	3	2					12		7		4	5	9*					36
1	11				6		8		10*	3	2					12		7		4	5	9					37
1					6		8			3	2					12	10	7*		4	5	9				11	38
1	11		4		6		8			3	2					10		7			5	9					39
1	11		4		6		8			3	2					10		7*			5	9			12		40
1	2				6		8			3						10	12	7		9	5				4*	11	41
1	2		4		6	12	8			3						9	10	7*			5					11	42
39	32	8	30	7	37	6	21	8	32	36	39	1	5	9	3	14	23	24	3	16	31	26	1	3	5	3	
						1	3			1	1			5		3	4		7				2	1	1		
	1		1		5		5	2	7		1	1	1			2	6			3	1	11					

57

1987-88

1	Aug	19	(a)	Tottenham H	L	1-3	McCreery	26,261
2		22	(a)	Sheffield W	W	1-0	Jackson D.	22,031
3		29	(h)	Nottingham F	L	0-1		20,111
4	Sep	1	(a)	Norwich C	D	1-1	Jackson P.	16,636
5		5	(h)	Wimbledon	L	1-2	McDonald (pen)	22,684
6		12	(a)	Manchester U	D	2-2	Mirandinha 2	45,137
7		20	(h)	Liverpool	L	1-4	McDonald (pen)	24,141
8		26	(h)	Southampton	W	2-1	Mirandinha, Goddard	18,093
9	Oct	3	(a)	Chelsea	D	2-2	Goddard, Wharton	22,071
10		17	(h)	Everton	D	1-1	Mirandinha	20,266
11		24	(a)	Coventry C	W	3-1	Goddard, Gascoigne, Jackson D.	18,585
12		31	(h)	Arsenal	L	0-1		23,662
13	Nov	7	(a)	Luton T	L	0-4		7,638
14		14	(h)	Derby Co	D	0-0		21,698
15		21	(a)	QPR	D	1-1	Jackson P.	11,794
16		28	(h)	Charlton A	W	2-1	Cornwell, Mirandinha	19,453
17	Dec	5	(a)	Oxford U	W	3-1	McDonald (pen), O'Neill, Mirandinha	8,190
18		12	(h)	Portsmouth	D	1-1	Mirandinha	20,455
19		19	(a)	West Ham U	L	1-2	Mirandinha	18,679
20		26	(h)	Manchester U	W	1-0	Roeder	26,461
21		28	(a)	Liverpool	L	0-4		44,637
22	Jan	1	(a)	Nottingham F	W	2-0	Gascoigne, Mirandinha	28,583
23		2	(h)	Sheffield W	D	2-2	Goddard 2	25,503
24		23	(h)	Tottenham H	W	2-0	Gascoigne 2	24,616
25	Feb	6	(a)	Wimbledon	D	0-0		10,505
26		13	(h)	Norwich C	L	1-3	Gascoigne	21,068
27		27	(h)	Chelsea	W	3-1	Mirandinha 2, Gascoigne	17,858
28	Mar	1	(a)	Southampton	D	1-1	O'Neill	13,380
29		5	(a)	Everton	L	0-1		25,674
30		19	(a)	Arsenal	D	1-1	Goddard	25,889
31		26	(h)	Coventry C	D	2-2	O'Neill 2	19,050
32	Apr	2	(h)	Luton T	W	4-0	O'Neill 3, Goddard	20,565
33		4	(a)	Derby Co	L	1-2	O'Neill	18,591
34		9	(h)	QPR	D	1-1	O'Neill	18,403
35		12	(h)	Watford	W	3-0	O'Neill, Wharton, Tinnion	16,318
36		19	(a)	Watford	D	1-1	Anderson	12,075
37		23	(a)	Charlton A	L	0-2		7,482
38		30	(h)	Oxford U	W	3-1	Lormor, O'Neill, Goddard	16,617
39	May	2	(a)	Portsmouth	W	2-1	Scott, Lormor	12,468
40		7	(h)	West Ham U	W	2-1	O'Neill, Gascoigne	23,731

FINAL LEAGUE POSITION: 8th in Division One

Appearances

Sub Appearances

Goals

Kelly	McDonald	Bailey	McCreery	Jackson P.	Roeder	Jackson D.	Gascoigne	Goddard	Wharton	Hodges	Thomas A.	Scott	Thomas M.	Anderson	Mirandinha	Timnion	Stephenson	Cornwell	O'Neill	Bogie	Craig	Lormor	#
1	2	3	4	5	6	7*	8	9	10	11	12												1
1	2	3	4	5		7	8	9	10	11		6											2
	2	3	4	5	6	7	8	9†	10*	11	14		1	12									3
	2		4	5	6	7	8		3	11			1	10	9								4
	2		4	5	6		8	9	3	11			1	7	10								5
1	2		4†	5	6	12		9	8	11*				3	10	14	7						6
1	2		4	5	6	12		9	8	11*				3	10		7						7
1	7		4	5	6	12	8	9						2*	10	3		11					8
1	7†		4	5	6	12	8	9	14					2	10	3		11*					9
1	2		4*	5	6	7	8	9	12						10	3		11					10
1	2		4	5	6	7	8	9	14					12	10*	3		11†					11
1	7		4	5	6	10	8	9						2		3		11					12
1	7			5	6	11	8	9	4					2	10	3*		12					13
1	7*			5	6	10	8	9	4					2		3		11	12				14
1	7		4	5	6		8		3					2	9					10	11		15
1	7		4	5	6				3					2	10			11	9				16
1	7		4	5	6				3					2	10			11	9	8			17
1	7		4	5	6			9	3					2	10			11		8			18
1	7		4	5	6	12	8	9						2	10	3*		11					19
1	2		4		6	7†	8	9	3*					5	10			11			14	12	20
1	2		4		6	7*	8	9	3					5	10			11			12		21
1	7		4	5	6		8	9	3					2	10			11					22
1	7		4	5	6	11	8	9	3					2*	10†			12				14	23
1	7			5	6	4	8	9	3					2	10*				11			12	24
1	7			5	6	4	8	9	3					2	10				11				25
1	7			5	6	4*	8	9	3					2	10			12	11				26
1	2		4	5	6	12	8	9	3						10*			7	11				27
1	2		4	5	6		8	9	3						10			7	11				28
1	7		4*	5	6	12	8	9						2	10	3			11				29
1	2		4		6	10	8	9						5		3	12	7*	11				30
1	2		4		6	10	8	9						5		3	7*	11	12				31
1	2		4		6		8	9	11					5			7		10				32
1	2†		4		6		8	9	11					5	14	3	7*	12	10				33
1	7		4	5	6	11	8	9	3					2					10				34
1	2		4		6	7*	8	9	11					5		3	12		10				35
1	2		4		6			9	3			7*		5	10†			12	11		14		36
1	2		4		6		8	12	9	11				5		3*		7	10				37
1	2		4		6	7*	8	9			12			5		3			10			11	38
1	2	12	4			7	8					6		5		3			10*			11	39
1	2		4			7	8	9				6		5		3			10†	12		11	40
37	40	3	35	28	37	24	34	35	28	7	1	4	3	33	25	15	5	20	19	3	1	3	
		1				7	1		3			3		2	1	1	2	4	2	4	2	2	
	3		1	2	1	2	7	8	2			1		1	11	1		1	12			2	

1988-89

1	Aug	27	(a)	Everton	L	0-4		41,560
2	Sep	3	(h)	Tottenham H	D	2-2	Thorn, Jackson D.	32,977
3		10	(a)	Derby Co	L	0-2		16,014
4		17	(h)	Norwich C	L	0-2		22,801
5		24	(a)	Charlton A	D	2-2	Jackson D., Tinnion	6,088
6	Oct	1	(a)	Liverpool	W	2-1	Hendrie, Mirandinha (pen)	39,139
7		8	(h)	Coventry C	L	0-3		22,896
8		22	(a)	West Ham U	L	0-2		17,765
9		26	(h)	Middlesbrough	W	3-0	Pallister (og), Mirandinha 2	23,927
10		29	(h)	Nottingham F	L	0-1		24,765
11	Nov	5	(a)	QPR	L	0-3		11,013
12		12	(h)	Arsenal	L	0-1		24,033
13		19	(a)	Millwall	L	0-4		15,767
14		27	(h)	Manchester U	D	0-0		20,350
15	Dec	3	(a)	Luton T	D	0-0		8,338
16		10	(h)	Wimbledon	W	2-1	Hendrie 2	20,146
17		17	(h)	Southampton	D	3-3	Brock, O'Neill 2	19,986
18		26	(a)	Sheffield W	W	2-1	McDonald, O'Neill	25,573
19		31	(a)	Tottenham H	L	0-2		27,739
20	Jan	2	(h)	Derby Co	L	0-1		30,555
21		14	(a)	Aston Villa	L	1-3	Mirandinha (pen)	21,010
22		21	(h)	Charlton A	L	0-2		19,076
23	Feb	4	(h)	Liverpool	D	2-2	Mirandinha, Pingel	30,966
24		11	(a)	Coventry C	W	2-1	Hendrie, Mirandinha (pen)	16,577
25		26	(a)	Middlesbrough	D	1-1	O'Brien	24,385
26	Mar	11	(h)	QPR	L	1-2	Ranson	21,577
27		15	(a)	Nottingham F	D	1-1	Brock	20,800
28		22	(h)	Everton	W	2-0	Mirandinha, O'Brien	20,933
29		25	(a)	Norwich C	W	2-0	Mirandinha, O'Brien	22,440
30		27	(h)	Sheffield W	L	1-3	Mirandinha (pen)	31,040
31	Apr	1	(a)	Southampton	L	0-1		16,175
32		8	(h)	Aston Villa	L	1-2	O'Brien	20,329
33		15	(a)	Arsenal	L	0-1		38,023
34		22	(h)	Luton T	D	0-0		18,493
35		29	(a)	Wimbledon	L	0-4		5,206
36	May	3	(h)	West Ham U	L	1-2	Lormor	14,202
37		6	(h)	Millwall	D	1-1	Anderson	14,435
38		13	(a)	Manchester U	L	0-2		30,379

FINAL LEAGUE POSITION: 20th in Division One

Appearances

Sub Appearances

Goals

Beasant	Anderson	Tinnion	McCreery	Jackson P.	Thorn	Hendrie	Robertson	Mirandinha	Wharton	O'Neill	Jackson D.	Scott	Bogie	Craig	Stephenson	Cornwell	Payne	Robinson	O'Brien	McDonald	Roeder	Gourlay	Brock	Ranson	Sansom	Wright	Pingel	Brazil	Kelly	Sweeney	Kristensen	Roche	Lormor	Howey	
1	2	3	4	5	6	7	8	9*	10	11	12																								1
1	2*		4		6	7	11		3	9	10	5	8	12																					2
1	2		4		6	7	11		3	9	10	5	8																						3
1	2	3	4		6	7	11			9*	10	5	8		12																				4
1		14	4		6	7	11†	9	3		10	5	12		8	2*																			5
1	2		4		6	7	12	9	3	10*	8	5				11																			6
1	2		4		6†	7	12	9	3	10*	8	5				11	14																		7
1	2	3	4*		6†	8	12	9		11	10	5	14		7																				8
1	2	3			8	12	9		10	4	5				7	6	11*																		9
1	2	3			8	12	9		10	4	5				7	6	11*																		10
1	2	3*	4		6	8	9		11	10	5				7		12																		11
1	2	3	4		6	8	7*	9		10						5	11	12																	12
1	2	3			6	8		12	11*		14					5†			7	9	10														13
1	2	3	4		6	7		10	12							5	11*		8	9															14
1	2	3	4		6	7		10*			9					5	11		8			12													15
1	2	3	4		6	7		10†	14		9*					5			8	12			11												16
1		3†	4		5	7		9*	10	12			14						2	8	6		11												17
1			4†		5	7		12	10	8*									14	9	6		11	2	3										18
1			4†			7		12	10	8*		5							14	9	6		11	2	3										19
1			4			7		9†	10*	12		5							14	8	6		11	2	3										20
			4			7		9	10			5					8*		6				11	2	3	1	12								21
	5		4†			7		12	10*	14									9		6		11	2	3	1	8								22
	5		4			7		9				2							10		6		11		3	1	8								23
	5		4			7		9*		12		2							10		6				3	1	8	11							24
			4			7		9*		5									10		6		11	2	3	1	8	12							25
			4			7*		12		14		5							10†		6		11	2	3	1	8	9							26
			4		6	7			14	12		5							10				11	2	3		8†	9*	1						27
			4		6	7		9†		14		5							10				11	2	3		8*	12	1						28
			4		6	7		9*		14		5							10				11	2	3		8†	12	1						29
			4		6	7		9		14		5							10				11	2†	3		8*	12	1						30
			4			7		9†		12		5							10		6		11	2	3		8*		1	14					31
			4			7		9*				5							10		6		11	2	3				1	12	8				32
			4		9	7				10		5									12	6			3		8*		1	11†	2	14			33
			4		9	7		12	14	10*		5									6		11		3				1	8	2†				34
			4		9					10		5									12	6	14		3		7*		1	8	2†				35
	2†		4		9							5									12	6			3	1	10*			8	14		7		36
	2		4		9			8	10			5									6		11		3	1							7		37
	2		4		6				10*			5									6		11		3	1					8	14	7†	12	38
20	21	12	36	1	26	34	7	22	14	17	13	29	3		7	8	6		17	6	18		21	13	20	9	13	3	9	6	4		3		
	1						5	6	4	10	2		3	1	1	1	1	1	3	4		1		1			1		4	2	1	2		1	
	1	1			1	4		9		3	2								4	1				2	1		1						1		

61

1989-90

1	Aug	19	(h)	Leeds U	W	5-2	Quinn 4 (1 pen), Gallacher		24,482
2		26	(a)	Leicester C	D	2-2	Quinn, Gallacher		13,384
3	Sep	2	(h)	Oldham A	W	2-1	Quinn 2 (1 pen)		20,804
4		9	(a)	Bournemouth	L	1-2	Quinn		9,882
5		13	(a)	Oxford U	L	1-2	Quinn		7,313
6		16	(h)	Portsmouth	W	1-0	Thorn		19,589
7		24	(a)	Sunderland	D	0-0			29,499
8		27	(h)	Watford	W	2-1	Gallacher, Quinn		17,040
9		30	(a)	Hull C	W	3-1	Anderson, Brazil, McGhee		9,629
10	Oct	7	(a)	Ipswich T	L	1-2	McGhee		13,679
11		14	(h)	Bradford C	W	1-0	McGhee		18,898
12		18	(h)	Blackburn R	W	2-1	McGhee, Quinn		20,702
13		21	(a)	Brighton & HA	W	3-0	Quinn 3		10,756
14		28	(h)	Port Vale	D	2-2	McGhee, Quinn		17,809
15	Nov	1	(a)	West Brom A	W	5-1	Robson (og), Brazil, Brock, McGhee, O'Brien		12,339
16		4	(h)	Middlesbrough	D	2-2	McGhee, O'Brien		23,349
17		11	(a)	West Ham U	D	0-0			25,892
18		18	(a)	Barnsley	D	1-1	Quinn		10,475
19		25	(h)	Sheffield U	W	2-0	Gallacher, Quinn		28,092
20	Dec	2	(a)	Leeds U	L	0-1			31,715
21		9	(h)	Oxford U	L	2-3	Stimson, Quinn (pen)		16,685
22		26	(a)	Stoke C	L	1-2	Scott		14,878
23		30	(a)	Swindon T	D	1-1	Quinn		11,657
24	Jan	1	(h)	Wolverhampton W	L	1-4	Brock		22,054
25		13	(h)	Leicester C	W	5-4	McGhee 2, Quinn 2, Gallacher		20,847
26		20	(a)	Oldham A	D	1-1	McGhee		11,194
27	Feb	4	(h)	Sunderland	D	1-1	McGhee		31,572
28		10	(a)	Portsmouth	D	1-1	Quinn		14,204
29		24	(a)	Sheffield U	D	1-1	Morris (og)		21,035
30		28	(h)	Bournemouth	W	3-0	Anderson, Quinn 2		15,119
31	Mar	3	(h)	Barnsley	W	4-1	Anderson, Scott, Aitken, McGhee (pen)		18,998
32		7	(h)	Hull C	W	2-0	McGhee 2 (1 pen)		20,499
33		10	(a)	Watford	D	0-0			12,069
34		17	(h)	Ipswich T	W	2-1	Quinn 2		19,521
35		21	(a)	Bradford C	L	2-3	McGhee (pen), Aizlewood (og)		10,264
36		24	(a)	Blackburn R	L	0-2			13,285
37		31	(h)	Brighton & HA	W	2-0	Gallacher, Quinn		18,746
38	Apr	3	(h)	Plymouth A	W	3-1	Quinn, McGhee 2 (1 pen)		16,558
39		7	(a)	Port Vale	W	2-1	Quinn, McGhee		10,290
40		11	(h)	West Brom A	W	2-1	Anderson, Quinn		19,460
41		14	(a)	Wolverhampton W	W	1-0	Scott		19,507
42		16	(h)	Stoke C	W	3-0	Kristensen 2, Quinn		26,190
43		21	(a)	Plymouth A	D	1-1	McGhee		11,702
44		25	(h)	Swindon T	D	0-0			26,568
45		28	(h)	West Ham U	W	2-1	Kristensen, Quinn		31,496
46	May	5	(a)	Middlesbrough	L	1-4	McGee (og)		18,484

FINAL LEAGUE POSITION: 3rd in Division Two

Appearances

Sub Appearances

Goals

Wright	Ranson	Sweeney	Dillon	Scott	Thorn	Gallacher	Brock	Quinn	McGhee	Fereday	Brazil	Stimson	Kristensen	Anderson	Kelly	Burridge	O'Brien	Bradshaw	Aitken	Robinson	Askew	
1	2	3*	4	5	6	7	8	9	10	11	12											1
1	2		4	5	6	7	8*	9	10	11		3	12									2
1	2†		4	5	6	7*	8	9	10	11	12	3	14									3
1	2	8*	4	5	6	7†		9	10	11		3	14	12								4
1	2		4*	5	6		8	9	10	11	7	3	12									5
	2			5	6	7	8	9	10	11		3	4*	12	1							6
			4	5	6	7*	8	9	10		12	3	11	2	1							7
			4	5	6	7	8	9	10	11		3		2	1							8
			4	5	6	7*	8	9†	10	11	12	3	14	2	1							9
			4	5	6†	7*	8	9	10	11	12	3	14	2		1						10
			4	5		7	8	9	10			3	6	2		1	11					11
			4	5		7*	8†	9	10	14	12	3	6	2		1	11					12
			4	5		7*	8	9	10	14	12	3	6	2†		1	11					13
	2		4	5			8	9	10	7		3	6			1	11					14
	2	14	4*	5			8	9	10	7	11†	3	6			1	12					15
	2†		4	5		14	8	9	10	7	11*	3	6			1	12					16
	2		4	5		14	8*	9	10		7†	3	6	12		1	11					17
	2*		4	5			8	9	10	7†	14	3	6	12		1	11					18
	2		4	5		7*	8	9	10	12		3	6			1	11					19
	2		4	5		7†	8	9	10	14		3*	6	12		1	11					20
	2	14	4*	5			8	9	10†	7		3	6	12		1	11					21
	2	3	4	5		7*	8	9	10		12†	14	6			1	11					22
		12		5			8	9	10	7*		3	6	2		1	11	4				23
				5		12	8	9	10	7		3	6	2		1	11	4*				24
		14	6†	5		12	8	9	10	7*		3		2		1	11		4			25
	7	3	6	5				9	10			8	2			1	11		4			26
	11†	8	5			7	14	9	10			3	6*	12		1	2		4			27
1	11	8	5			7		9	10			3	6*	12			2		4			28
1	6		8			7		9	10	11		3		5			2		4			29
1	6		8			7		9	10	11		3		5			2		4			30
1	6		8	2		12	7	9	10	11*		3		5					4			31
1	6	12	8	2		11	7	9	10			3*		5					4			32
1	6	3	8	2		11	7	9	10					5					4			33
1	6	3	8*			11†	7	9	10		12			5			2		4	14		34
1	6	3	8†			11*	7	9	10		12		14	5			2		4			35
1	6	3†	8	2			7	9	10		12			5				14*	4		11	36
	6		8	2		12	7*	9	10			3		5		1			4		11	37
	6		8	2		12	7*	9	10				14	5†		1			4		11	38
	6		8	2			7	9	10			3		5		1			4		11	39
	6		8	2			7	9	10	11*	12			5		1			4			40
	6		8	2			7	9	10			3	11	5		1			4			41
	6†		8*	2			7	9	10			3	11	5		1	12	14	4			42
			8	2			7	9	10			3	11	5		1		6	4			43
	6		8	2			7	9	10			3	11	5		1			4			44
	6		8*	2			7	9	10			3	11	5		1	12		4			45
	6		8	2†			7	9*	10			3	11	5		1	12	14	4			46
14	33	14	43	42	10	21	43	45	46	21	4	35	25	29	4	28	14	9	22		4	
		5				7	1			4	12	2	8	8			5	3		1		
			3	1	6	2	32	19		2	1	3	4				2		1			

1990-91

#	Month	Date		Opponent	Result	Score	Scorers	Attendance
1	Aug	25	(h)	Plymouth A	W	2-0	Kristensen, Quinn	23,984
2	Sep	1	(a)	Blackburn R	W	1-0	O'Brien	11,329
3		8	(h)	Millwall	L	1-2	Quinn	23,922
4		15	(a)	Port Vale	W	1-0	Quinn	10,025
5		18	(a)	Sheffield W	D	2-2	McGhee 2	30,628
6		22	(h)	West Ham U	D	1-1	McGhee	25,462
7		29	(a)	Bristol C	L	0-1		15,858
8	Oct	3	(h)	Middlesbrough	D	0-0		17,023
9		6	(h)	Portsmouth	W	2-1	Quinn 2	17,682
10		13	(a)	Oxford U	D	0-0		6,820
11		20	(a)	Ipswich T	L	1-2	Quinn (pen)	15,567
12		24	(h)	Charlton A	L	1-3	Brock	14,016
13		27	(h)	West Brom A	D	1-1	O'Brien	14,774
14	Nov	3	(a)	Hull C	L	1-2	McGhee	8,375
15		10	(a)	Wolverhampton W	L	1-2	Clark	18,721
16		17	(h)	Barnsley	D	0-0		15,548
17		24	(h)	Watford	W	1-0	Quinn (pen)	13,774
18	Dec	1	(a)	Leicester C	L	4-5	Quinn 3, O'Brien	11,045
19		16	(a)	Plymouth A	W	1-0	Peacock	7,845
20		22	(a)	Bristol R	D	1-1	Gaynor	6,643
21		26	(h)	Swindon T	D	1-1	Quinn	17,003
22		29	(h)	Notts Co	L	0-2		17,557
23	Jan	1	(a)	Oldham A	D	1-1	Quinn	14,550
24		12	(h)	Blackburn R	W	1-0	Mitchell	16,382
25		16	(a)	Brighton & HA	L	2-4	Quinn, Brock	7,684
26		19	(a)	Millwall	W	1-0	Peacock	11,478
27	Feb	2	(h)	Port Vale	W	2-0	Peacock, Quinn	14,602
28		23	(h)	Wolverhampton W	D	0-0		18,612
29		27	(h)	Brighton & HA	D	0-0		12,692
30	Mar	2	(h)	Leicester C	W	2-1	McGhee, Sloan	13,575
31		9	(a)	Watford	W	2-1	Anderson, Quinn	10,018
32		12	(a)	Middlesbrough	L	0-3		18,250
33		16	(h)	Bristol C	D	0-0		13,578
34		23	(a)	Portsmouth	W	1-0	Brock	9,607
35		30	(a)	Swindon T	L	2-3	Peacock, Quinn	9,309
36	Apr	1	(h)	Bristol R	L	0-2		17,509
37		6	(a)	Notts Co	L	0-3		7,806
38		10	(h)	Oxford U	D	2-2	Hunt, Melville (og)	10,004
39		13	(h)	Oldham A	W	3-2	Peacock, Hunt, Brock	16,615
40		17	(h)	Sheffield W	W	1-0	Brock	18,330
41		20	(h)	Ipswich T	D	2-2	Stimson, Quinn	17,638
42		24	(a)	West Ham U	D	1-1	Peacock	24,195
43		27	(a)	Charlton A	L	0-1		7,234
44	May	4	(a)	West Brom A	D	1-1	Quinn	16,706
45		7	(a)	Barnsley	D	1-1	Peacock	9,534
46		11	(h)	Hull C	L	1-2	Clark	17,940

FINAL LEAGUE POSITION: 11th in Division Two

Appearances

Sub Appearances

Goals

Burridge	Scott	Sweeney	Aitken	Kristensen	Ranson	Dillon	Anderson	Quinn	Howey	O'Brien	McGhee	Brock	Fereday	Simpson	Bradshaw	Gourlay	Gallacher	Clark	Robinson	Sloan	Appleby	Askew	Roche	Watson S.	Stimson	Gaynor	Peacock	Mitchell	Makel	Moran	Hunt	Watson J.	Neilson	Elliott	Smicek	
1	2	3	4	5	6	7	8	9	10	11																										1
1	2	3	4	5	6	7	8	9	12	11	10*																									2
1	2	3	4	5	6	7*	8	9	12	11†	10	14																								3
1	2		4	5	6	7*	3	9		11	10	8†	12	14																						4
1	2			5	6	7	3	9			10	8	11	12	4*																					5
1	2		4	5	6	7	3*	9		14	10	8†	11	12																						6
1	2		4	5	6			9		10			8*	3	7	11†	12	14																		7
1	2	3	4	5*	6	7		9		11	10	8						12																		8
1	2	3	4		6	7*	5	9		11	10	8						12																		9
1	2		4		6		5	9		11	10	8	7*			3		12																		10
1	2	3	4	10	14		5	9		11*		8	7			6†		12																		11
1	2	14	4*	5	6		3†	9		11	10	8						12		7																12
1	2	3		5	6			12	11	10		9†			8					7*	4	14														13
1	2				6		5	9		11	10	9*				7	8									12										14
1	2				6		5	9		11*	10		3	4		7	8									12										15
1	2				6		3	9		11		8	12	4*		7	10							5												16
1	2		4	5	6			9		11		8								10				3	7											17
1	2		4	5				9		11		8						12		10				3	7*	6										18
1	5		4	6†	14	2		9	12			11								7*				3	10		8									19
1	5		4	6	12	2		9	7			11*												3	10		8									20
1	5		4	6	8	11	2	9	12			7								10*				3												21
1	5		4*	6	10	11	2	9	12			7†								14				3			8									22
1	5		4	6	2			9	12			7								10			11*	3			8									23
1			4	6	2	7	5	9			12												11	3			8*	10								24
1			4	6	5	10						7						12					11	3			8*									25
1			4	6	2	7*	5	9			12	11											10	3			8									26
1			4	6	2	7	5	9				11											10	3			8									27
1	5		4	6	2	7		9			12	11†											14	3			8			10*						28
1	5		4	6	2	7		9			12	11											10	3			8*									29
1	5		4	6			2	9			12	10	11					7*						3			8									30
1	5		4	6		2†		9	7		10*	11												3			8				12	14				31
1	5		4	6				9	7			11†						12						3			8*			10		2	14			32
1	5		4	6				9	10†	12	14	11												2			8*			7		3				33
1	5		4	6		7		9		14	10*	11†												2	3		8				12					34
1	5		4			7		9				11												2	3		8				10					35
1	5		4	14		7†	6	9			12	11												2	3		8				10*					36
1	5		4	6		7*		9			10†	11						12						2	3		8				14					37
1	5			6				9				11						7	12				4	2	3		8				10*					38
1	5			6				9				11						7	12				4	2	3		8				10*					39
	5			6				9	12	14		11						7†					4†	2	3		8				10*				1	40
	5			6				9	12	14		11						7					4†	2	3		8				10*				1	41
	5			6				9			4	11						7						2			8				10			3	1	42
	5			6				9	12		4	11						7†					14	2			8				10*			3	1	43
	5			6				9	12		4							7					11	2†			8	14			10*			3	1	44
	5			6				9	12		4							7					14				8	11			10*			3†	1	45
	5			6				9			4	11						7						2			8	12			10*	14		3†	1	46
39	42	8	32	39	24	19	27	43	3	23	17	36	6	1	6	2	1	13		11	1	1	5	22	23	4	27	2								
		1		1	3				8	10	4	2	2	2	3	1		6	3	5		1	3	2								1	1	7	1	
		1					1	18		3	5	5						2		1				1	1		7	1								

1991-92

#	Month	Date		Opponent	Result	Score	Scorers	Attendance
1	Aug	18	(a)	Charlton A	L	1-2	Carr	9,322
2		24	(h)	Watford	D	2-2	Hunt, Clark	22,440
3		27	(a)	Middlesbrough	L	0-3		16,970
4		31	(a)	Bristol R	W	2-1	O'Brien, Quinn	6,334
5	Sep	4	(h)	Plymouth A	D	2-2	Carr, Quinn	19,543
6		7	(a)	Tranmere R	L	2-3	O'Brien, Clark	11,465
7		14	(h)	Wolverhampton W	L	1-2	Madden (og)	20,195
8		17	(h)	Ipswich T	D	1-1	Quinn (pen)	16,336
9		21	(a)	Millwall	L	1-2	Neilson	9,156
10		28	(h)	Derby Co	D	2-2	Hunt, Quinn	17,581
11	Oct	5	(a)	Portsmouth	L	1-3	Quinn	10,175
12		12	(h)	Leicester C	W	2-0	Hunt, Clark	16,966
13		19	(h)	Oxford U	W	4-3	Hunt, Peacock	16,454
14		26	(a)	Bristol C	D	1-1	Clark	8,613
15	Nov	2	(a)	Swindon T	L	1-2	Peacock	10,731
16		6	(h)	Cambridge U	D	1-1	Hunt	13,077
17		9	(h)	Grimsby T	W	2-0	Hunt, Howey	16,959
18		17	(a)	Sunderland	D	1-1	O'Brien	29,224
19		20	(h)	Southend U	W	3-2	Peacock 2 (1 pen), Hunt	14,740
20		23	(h)	Blackburn R	D	0-0		23,639
21		30	(a)	Barnsley	L	0-3		9,648
22	Dec	7	(h)	Port Vale	D	2-2	Makel, Peacock (pen)	18,162
23		14	(a)	Brighton & HA	D	2-2	Peacock, Kelly	7,658
24		20	(a)	Plymouth A	L	0-2		5,048
25		26	(h)	Middlesbrough	L	0-1		26,563
26		28	(h)	Bristol R	W	2-1	Brock, Kelly	19,329
27	Jan	1	(a)	Southend U	L	0-4		9,458
28		11	(a)	Watford	D	2-2	Kelly, Hunt	9,811
29		18	(h)	Charlton A	L	3-4	Clark, Hunt, Brock	15,663
30	Feb	1	(a)	Oxford U	L	2-5	Scott, Peacock (pen)	5,872
31		8	(h)	Bristol C	W	3-0	Kelly 2, O'Brien	29,263
32		15	(a)	Blackburn R	L	1-3	Kelly	19,511
33		22	(h)	Barnsley	D	1-1	Kelly	27,670
34		29	(a)	Port Vale	W	1-0	Watson S.	10,321
35	Mar	7	(h)	Brighton & HA	L	0-1		24,597
36		10	(a)	Cambridge U	W	2-0	Peacock, Kelly	8,254
37		14	(h)	Swindon T	W	3-1	Kelly, Peacock, Quinn	23,138
38		21	(a)	Grimsby T	D	1-1	Sheedy	11,613
39		29	(h)	Sunderland	W	1-0	Kelly	30,306
40		31	(a)	Wolverhampton W	L	2-6	Quinn, Peacock	14,480
41	Apr	4	(h)	Tranmere R	L	2-3	Brock 2	21,125
42		11	(a)	Ipswich T	L	2-3	Peacock 2	20,673
43		18	(h)	Millwall	L	0-1		23,821
44		20	(a)	Derby Co	L	1-4	Peacock	21,363
45		25	(h)	Portsmouth	W	1-0	Kelly	25,989
46	May	2	(a)	Leicester C	W	2-1	Peacock, Walsh (og)	21,861

FINAL LEAGUE POSITION: 20th in Division Two

Appearances

Sub Appearances

Goals

Srnicek	Watson S	Elliott	O'Brien	Scott	Bradshaw	Clark	Peacock	Quinn	Carr	Brock	Roche	Robinson	Hunt	Neilson	Makel	Stimson	Howey	Walker	Appleby	Maguire	Wright	Thompson	Bodin	Kelly	Wilson	Ranson	Kilcline	Sheedy	McDonough	Kristensen	Garland	No.
1	2†	3	4	5	6	7	8	9	10	11*	12	14																				1
1	2	3	4	5	6	7	8	9	10				11																			2
1	12	3	4†	5	6	7	8	9	10			14	11*	2																		3
1		3	4	5	6	7	8	9	10	11*				2	12																	4
1		3	4	5	6	7	8†	9	10	11*			14	2	12																	5
1	2	3	4	5	6	7	8	9	10	11*	12																					6
1		3	4	5	6	7	2	9	10	8			11																			7
1			4	5	6	7	2	9	10*	8	12		11†			3	14															8
1			4	5	6	7	8	9		11			12	2		3		10*														9
1		3	4	5	6†	7	8	9		11	14		12	2				10*														10
1			4	5	6	7	8	9	12		11†		10*	2		3			14													11
1			4	5		7	8		11†	12	9*		10	2		3	14		6													12
			4	5		7	8			11	12		10*	2		3	9		6		1											13
			4	5		7	8*			11	12		10	2†	14	3	9		6		1											14
			4	5	2	7	8			11			10*			3	9		6		1	12										15
			4	5	2*	7	8			10	11		14			3†	9		6		1	12										16
	12		4	5			8			10*	2		11			3	9		6		1	7										17
	12		4	5	2*		8			7			11	14		3	9		6		1	10†										18
	2		4	5	14		8			12	7		10*			3†	9		6		1	11										19
	2	3	4	5			8			12	7		10				9		6		1	11*										20
	2		4	5	14		8			12	7		10			3	9		6†		1	11*										21
			4	5			8			11	2		10	7					6		1		3	9								22
	12		4*	5			8			11	2		10	7					6		1		3	9								23
	12			5	2*		8			11	4		10	7		14			6		1		3	9								24
	2			5	12		8			11	4*		10	7		14			6		1		3	9								25
	2			5	7		8			11			10*				12		6		1	4	3	9								26
	2			5	7		8						12		11		10		6		1	4	3	9*								27
			4	5	3*	7	8						10				12		6		1	11		9								28
			4	5		7	8			11	14		10†				12		6		1	3		9*								29
			4	5		7	8			11			10†	2		3*	12	14			1			9	6							30
	7		4	5			8			11	12					6	3				1			9	10*	2						31
	7		4	5	10		8			12	11					6	3				1			9		2*						32
	2		4		10*		8			12	11	14				6	3				1			9			5	7†				33
	7		4		6	12	8			10*	11			2			3				1			9			5					34
	7*		4		6		8			12	11					3			2		1			9			5	10				35
	2		4		6	7	8				11						12				1	3		9			5	10				36
	2		4		6	7	8				11						12				1	3*		9			5	10				37
	2				6	7	8				11					3					1			9		12	5	10	4*			38
	2		4		6	7	8				11					3					1			9			5	10				39
	2		4		6	7	8				11					3					1			9			5*	10	12			40
1	2				6	12	8	7			11					3								9			5	10	4*			41
			4		6	7*	8			12	11					3					1			9		2†	5	10			14	42
			4		6	7*	8			12	11					3					1			9			5	10		2†	14	43
	2		4		6		8	7*			11					3					1			9			5	10				44
			4		6		8	12	7	11*						3					1			9		2	5	10				45
			4		6	12	8	7		11*						3†					1			9		2	5	10			14	46
13	23	9	40	44	17	25	46	18	12	31	18		21	16	5	23	13	2	16	3	33	12	6	25	2	5	12	13	2	1		
	5			2	4		4	3	4	8	3	6		4	1	8		2				2			1			1	1	1	2	
1			4	1		5	16	7	2	4			9	1	1		1					11						1				

1992-93

1	Aug	15	(h)	Southend U	W	3-2	Bracewell, Prior (og), Clark	28,545
2		22	(a)	Derby Co	W	2-1	Peacock, Clark	17,522
3		29	(h)	West Ham U	W	2-0	Peacock, Kelly	29,855
4	Sep	2	(h)	Luton T	W	2-0	Clark, Kelly	27,054
5		5	(a)	Bristol R	W	2-1	Sheedy, O'Brien	7,487
6		12	(h)	Portsmouth	W	3-1	Quinn 2, Kelly	29,885
7		19	(h)	Bristol C	W	5-0	O'Brien, Peacock 2 (2 pens), Carr, Brock	29,465
8		26	(a)	Peterborough U	W	1-0	Sheedy	14,487
9	Oct	4	(a)	Brentford	W	2-1	Kelly, Peacock	10,131
10		13	(h)	Tranmere R	W	1-0	Kelly	30,137
11		18	(a)	Sunderland	W	2-1	Owers (og), O'Brien	28,098
12		24	(h)	Grimsby T	L	0-1		30,088
13		31	(a)	Leicester C	L	1-2	O'Brien	19,687
14	Nov	4	(a)	Birmingham C	W	3-2	Peacock, Scott, Matthewson (og)	14,376
15		8	(h)	Swindon T	D	0-0		28,091
16		14	(a)	Charlton A	W	3-1	Peacock 2, Howey	12,945
17		21	(h)	Watford	W	2-0	Peacock, Lee	28,871
18		28	(h)	Cambridge U	W	4-1	Kelly 3, Peacock	27,991
19	Dec	5	(a)	Notts Co	W	2-0	Sheedy, Peacock	14,840
20		13	(a)	Barnsley	L	0-1		13,263
21		20	(h)	Millwall	D	1-1	Kelly (pen)	26,089
22		26	(h)	Wolverhampton W	W	2-1	Kelly 2	30,137
23		28	(a)	Oxford U	L	2-4	O'Brien, Clark	9,293
24	Jan	9	(a)	Bristol C	W	2-1	Kelly, Scott	15,446
25		16	(h)	Peterborough U	W	3-0	Lee 2, Kelly	29,155
26		20	(a)	Southend U	D	1-1	Peacock	8,246
27		27	(a)	Luton T	D	0-0		10,237
28		31	(h)	Derby Co	D	1-1	O'Brien	27,285
29	Feb	9	(a)	Portsmouth	L	0-2		21,028
30		21	(a)	West Ham U	D	0-0		24,159
31		24	(h)	Bristol R	D	0-0		29,372
32		28	(a)	Tranmere R	W	3-0	Lee 2, Kelly	13,082
33	Mar	6	(h)	Brentford	W	5-1	Kelly, Bracewell, Clark 2, Lee	30,006
34		10	(h)	Charlton A	D	2-2	Lee, Kelly	29,582
35		13	(a)	Swindon T	L	1-2	Kelly	17,574
36		20	(h)	Notts Co	W	4-0	Lee, Kelly 2, Cole	30,029
37		23	(a)	Watford	L	0-1		11,634
38		28	(h)	Birmingham C	D	2-2	Cole, Lee	27,087
39	Apr	3	(a)	Cambridge U	W	3-0	Howey, Kelly, Cole	7,925
40		7	(h)	Barnsley	W	6-0	Cole 3, Clark, Beresford, Sellars	29,460
41		10	(a)	Wolverhampton W	L	0-1		17,244
42		17	(a)	Millwall	W	2-1	Clark, Cole	14,262
43		25	(h)	Sunderland	W	1-0	Sellars	30,364
44	May	4	(a)	Grimsby T	W	2-0	Kelly, Cole	14,402
45		6	(h)	Oxford U	W	2-1	Clark, Cole	29,438
46		9	(h)	Leicester C	W	7-1	Cole 3, Lee, Kelly 3	30,129

FINAL LEAGUE POSITION: 1st in Division One

Appearances

Sub Appearances

Goals

Wright	Venison	Beresford	Bracewell	Kilcline	Howey	Watson	Peacock	Kelly	Clark	Sheedy	Scott	Carr	Ranson	O'Brien	Quinn	Thompson	Brock	Lee	Neilson	Srnicek	Stimson	Robinson	Sellars	Cole	No.
1	2	3	4	5	6	7	8	9	10	11															1
1	2	3		5	4		8	9	10	11	6	7													2
1	2				6		8	9	10	11	5	7	3	4											3
1	2				6		8	9	10	11	5	7	3	4											4
1	2		12†	13	6		8*	9	10	11	5	7	3	4											5
1	2	3						9*	10	11	5	7		4	8	12									6
1	2	3			6		8	9	10	11*	5	7†		4	12		13								7
1	2	3			6			9	10	11	5			4	8*		12	7							8
1	2	3			6		8	9	10	11	5			4				7							9
1	2	3			6		8	9	10		5			4	11			7							10
1	2	3			6		8	9	10		5			4			11	7							11
1	2*	3	13	12	6		8		10		5			4	9		11†	7							12
1		3		12	6		8	9	10	11	5			4			7*		2						13
1*	2	3		13	6		8	9	10	11†	5	7		4			12								14
	2	3			6		8	9	10	11	5	7		4						1					15
	2	3	11		6		8	9	10		5			4				7		1					16
	2	3	11	12	6*		8	9	10		5	13		4				7†		1					17
	2	3			6		8	9	10		5			4			11	7		1					18
	2	3			6		8	9	10	11	5			4				7		1					19
	2	3			6		8	9	10	11	5			4				7		1					20
	2	3*	8	12	6			9	10	11†	5	13		4				7		1					21
	2				6		8	9	10	11	5			4				7	3	1					22
	2	3		12	6		8*	9	10	11	5			4				7		1					23
	2	3	12		6		8	9	10	11*	5			4				7		1					24
	2	3	12		6		8	9	10	11*	5			4				7		1					25
	2	3			6		8	9	10		5			4			11	7		1					26
	2	3	11		6		8	9	10		5			4				7		1					27
	2	3	12	13	6		8	9†	10	11*	5			4				7		1					28
	2	3	11*	5			8	9	10	12	6			4				7		1					29
	2	3			6		8	9	10	11	5			4				7		1					30
	2	3			6	12	8	9	10	11*	5			4				7		1					31
	2	3	13	12†	6		8	9	10	11	5*			4				7		1					32
	2	3	8		6*			9	10		5			4				7	12	1	11				33
		3	8		6			9	10		5			4				7		1	12	2	11*		34
	2	3	8		6			9	10		5			4*				7		1		11	12		35
	2	3	4		6	13		9	10†		5*							7		1		12	11	8	36
	2	3	4		6			9	10		5							7		1		12	11*	8	37
	2	3	4		6			9	10		5							7		1			11	8	38
	2	3	4*		6			9	10		5							7		1		12	11	8	39
	2	3	4*	13	6†			9	10		5							7		1		12	11	8	40
	2	3	4	13	6			9†	10		5							7		1		12	11*	8	41
	2	3	4	6				9	10		5							7		1			11	8*	42
	2	3	4		6			9	10		5							7		1			11	8	43
	2	3	4		6			9	10		5							7		1			11	8	44
	2	3	4†	6		13		9	10		5							7*		1		12	11	8	45
	2	3*		13	6†	12		9	10		5							7		1		4	11	8	46
14	44	42	19	7	41	1	29	45	46	23	45	8	3	33	4	1	4	36	2	32	1	2	13	11	
			6	12	1	3				1		2			1	1	3		1		1	7		1	
		1	2		2		12	24	9	3	2	1		6	2		1	10				2		12	

1993-94

1	Aug	14	(h)	Tottenham H	L	0-1		34,565
2		18	(a)	Coventry C	L	1-2	Atherton (og)	15,763
3		21	(a)	Manchester U	D	1-1	Cole	41,829
4		25	(h)	Everton	W	1-0	Allen	34,490
5		29	(h)	Blackburn R	D	1-1	Cole	33,987
6		31	(a)	Ipswich T	D	1-1	Cole	19,126
7	Sep	13	(h)	Sheffield W	W	4-2	Cole 2, Mathie, Allen	33,519
8		18	(a)	Swindon T	D	2-2	Clark, Allen (pen)	15,393
9		25	(h)	West Ham U	W	2-0	Cole 2	34,179
10	Oct	2	(a)	Aston Villa	W	2-0	Allen (pen), Cole	37,366
11		16	(h)	QPR	L	1-2	Allen	33,801
12		24	(a)	Southampton	L	1-2	Cole	13,804
13		30	(h)	Wimbledon	W	4-0	Beardsley 3 (1 pen), Cole	33,371
14	Nov	8	(a)	Oldham Ath	W	3-1	Cole 2, Beardsley	13,821
15		21	(h)	Liverpool	W	3-0	Cole 3	36,246
16		24	(h)	Sheffield U	W	4-0	Ward (og), Beardsley 2 (1 pen), Cole	35,029
17		27	(a)	Arsenal	L	1-2	Beardsley	36,091
18	Dec	4	(a)	Tottenham H	W	2-1	Beardsley 2	30,780
19		11	(h)	Manchester U	D	1-1	Cole	36,332
20		18	(a)	Everton	W	2-0	Cole, Beardsley	25,362
21		22	(h)	Leeds U	D	1-1	Cole	36,388
22		28	(a)	Chelsea	L	0-1		23,133
23	Jan	1	(h)	Manchester C	W	2-0	Cole 2	35,585
24		4	(a)	Norwich C	W	2-1	Beadsley, Cole	19,564
25		16	(a)	QPR	W	2-1	Clark, Beardsley	15,774
26		22	(h)	Southampton	L	1-2	Cole	32,067
27	Feb	12	(a)	Wimbledon	L	2-4	Beardsley 2 (2 pens)	13,358
28		19	(a)	Blackburn R	L	0-1		20,798
29		23	(h)	Coventry C	W	4-0	Cole 3, Mathie	32,210
30	Mar	5	(a)	Sheffield W	W	1-0	Cole	33,153
31		12	(h)	Swindon T	W	7-1	Beardsley 2 (1 pen), Lee 2, Watson 2, Fox	32,219
32		19	(a)	West Ham U	W	4-2	Lee 2, Cole, Mathie	23,132
33		23	(h)	Ipswich T	W	2-0	Sellars, Cole	32,234
34		29	(h)	Norwich C	W	3-0	Cole, Lee, Beardsley	32,228
35	Apr	1	(a)	Leeds U	D	1-1	Cole	40,005
36		4	(h)	Chelsea	D	0-0		32,218
37		9	(a)	Manchester C	L	1-2	Sellars	33,774
38		16	(a)	Liverpool	W	2-0	Lee, Cole	44,601
39		23	(h)	Oldham Ath	W	3-2	Fox, Beardsley, Lee	32,214
40		27	(h)	Aston Villa	W	5-1	Bracewell, Beardsley 2 (1 pen), Cole, Sellars	32,217
41		30	(a)	Sheffield U	L	0-2		29,013
42	May	7	(h)	Arsenal	W	2-0	Cole, Beardsley (pen)	32,216

FINAL LEAGUE POSITION: 3rd in the F.A. Premiership

Appearances

Sub. Appearances

Goals

Srnicek	Venison	Beresford	Bracewell	Scott	Howey	Lee	Allen	Cole	Clark	Papavasiliou	O'Brien	Watson	Wright	Neilson	Mathie	Beardsley	Hooper	Sellars	Elliott	Jeffrey	Robinson	Kildine	Fox	Appleby	Holland	Peacock	
1	2	3	4	5	6	7	8†	9	10	11*	12	14															1
1	2	3	4	5		7		9	10	11*	6	8	12														2
1	2	3	4	5		7		9	10	11	6	8															3
1	2	3	4	5			8	9	10	11	6	7															4
1	2	3	4	5		7		9	10	11	6	8															5
1	2	3	4	5		7	8	9	10*	11†	12	6		14													6
	2	3	4	5		7	8	9	10	11*		6	1		12												7
	2	3	4	5		7	11	9	10			6	1			8											8
	2	3	4	5		7	11	9	10			6				8	1										9
	2	3	4	5		7	11	9	10			6				8	1										10
	2	3	4	5		7	11	9	10			6				8	1										11
	2	3	4	5		7	11†	9	10*			6			12	8	1	14									12
	2	3	4	5		7		9	10			6				8	1	11									13
	2		4	5		7		9	10			6				8	1	11	3								14
	2		4	5		7		9	10			6				8	1	11	3								15
	2		4*	5		7		9	10			6			12	8	1	11	3								16
	2		4	5	14	7		9	10†			6			12	8	1	11	3*								17
	2		4		5	7		9	10			6				8	1		3	11							18
	2		4		5	7		9	10			6				8	1	11	3								19
	2	3*	4		5	7		9	10			6				8	1	11	12								20
	2	3	4		5	7		9	10*			6			12	8	1	11									21
	2	3	4		5	7		9	10*			6†			12	8	1	11			14						22
		3	4†		6	7		9	10			14			12	8	1	11			2*	5					23
		3		5	6	7		9	10							8	1	11	4		2						24
	2	3	4		6	7		9	10							8	1	11			5						25
	2	3	4		6	7		9	10							8	1	11			5						26
	2	3		5	9*				10			6			12	8	1	11	4				7				27
1	2	3		5	9				10			6				8		11	4				7				28
1						7†		9	10			2	5	12		8		11*	3		14		6	4			29
1		3	4*			7		9				6		5	12	8		11			2		10				30
1	4	3				7		9				6				8		11	5		2		10				31
1	4	3				7		9				6†		14	12	8		11	5		2		10*				32
1	4	3				7		9				6*		14	12	8		11	5†		2		10				33
1		3	4†			7		9				6			12	8		11			2		10*		14	5	34
1	12	3	4			7*		9				6				8		11			2		10			5	35
1	6	3†	4			7		9						14	12	8		11			2				10*	5	36
1	3					7		9				6			12	8		11		10*	2		4			5	37
1	2†	3	4			7		9				6			12	8*		11		14			10			5	38
1	2	3	4			7		9				6				8		11					10			5	39
1	2	3	4†			7		9*	14			6			12	8		11					10			5	40
1	2	3	4			7		9				6				8		11					10			5	41
1	2	3				7		9			4*	6			12	8		11					10			5	42
21	36	34	32	18	13	41	9	40	29	7	4	29	2	10		35	19	29	13	2	12	1	14	1	2	9	
	1		1								2	3	1	4	16		1	2	4				1				
			1			7	5	34	2			2			3	21		3					2				

1994-95

1	Aug	21	(a)	Leicester C	W	3-1	Cole, Beardsley, Elliott	20,048
2		24	(h)	Coventry C	W	4-0	Lee 2, Watson, Cole	34,163
3		27	(h)	Southampton	W	5-1	Watson 2, Cole 2, Lee	34,182
4		31	(a)	West Ham U	W	3-1	Potts (og), Lee, Mathie	17,375
5	Sep	10	(h)	Chelsea	W	4-2	Cole 2, Fox, Lee	34,435
6		18	(a)	Arsenal	W	3-2	Keown (og), Beardsley (pen), Fox	36,819
7		24	(h)	Liverpool	D	1-1	Lee	34,435
8	Oct	1	(a)	Aston Villa	W	2-0	Lee, Cole	29,960
9		9	(h)	Blackburn R	D	1-1	Flowers (og)	34,344
10		15	(a)	Crystal Palace	W	1-0	Beardsley	17,739
11		22	(h)	Sheffield W	W	2-1	Watson, Cole	34,369
12		29	(a)	Manchester U	L	0-2		43,795
13	Nov	5	(h)	QPR	W	2-1	Kitson, Beardsley	34,278
14		7	(a)	Nottingham F	D	0-0		22,102
15		19	(a)	Wimbledon	L	2-3	Beardsley, Kitson	14,203
16		26	(h)	Ipswich T	D	1-1	Cole	34,459
17	Dec	3	(a)	Tottenham H	L	2-4	Fox 2	28,002
18		10	(h)	Leicester C	W	3-1	Albert 2, Howey	34,400
19		17	(a)	Coventry C	D	0-0		17,237
20		26	(a)	Leeds U	D	0-0		39,337
21		31	(a)	Norwich C	L	1-2	Fox (pen)	21,172
22	Jan	2	(h)	Manchester C	D	0-0		34,437
23		15	(h)	Manchester U	D	1-1	Kitson	34,471
24		21	(a)	Sheffield W	D	0-0		31,215
25		25	(h)	Wimbledon	W	2-1	Fox, Kitson	34,374
26	Feb	1	(h)	Everton	W	2-0	Fox, Beardsley (pen)	34,465
27		4	(a)	QPR	L	0-3		16,576
28		11	(h)	Nottingham F	W	2-1	Fox, Lee	34,471
29		25	(h)	Aston Villa	W	3-1	Venison, Beardsley 2	34,637
30		28	(a)	Ipswich T	W	2-0	Fox, Kitson	18,639
31	Mar	4	(a)	Liverpool	L	0-2		39,300
32		8	(h)	West Ham U	W	2-0	Clark, Kitson	34,595
33		19	(h)	Arsenal	W	1-0	Beardsley	35,611
34		22	(a)	Southampton	L	1-3	Kitson	14,666
35	Apr	1	(a)	Chelsea	D	1-1	Hottiger	22,987
36		8	(h)	Norwich C	W	3-0	Beardsley 2 (1 pen), Kitson	35,518
37		14	(a)	Everton	L	0-2		34,628
38		17	(h)	Leeds U	L	1-2	Elliott	35,626
39		29	(a)	Manchester C	D	0-0		27,389
40	May	3	(h)	Tottenham H	D	3-3	Gillespie, Peacock, Beardsley	35,603
41		8	(a)	Blackburn R	L	0-1		30,545
42		14	(h)	Crystal Palace	W	3-2	Fox, Lee, Gillespie	35,626

FINAL LEAGUE POSITION: 6th in the F.A. Premiership

Appearances

Sub. Appearances

Goals

Srnicek	Hottiger	Beresford	Venison	Peacock	Albert	Lee	Beardsley	Cole	Fox	Sellars	Elliott	Mathie	Hooper	Watson	Howey	Kitson	Neilson	Clark	Bracewell	Gillespie	Allen	#
1	2	3	4	5	6	7	8†	9	10	11*	12	14°	15									1
1	2	3	4	5	6	7		9	10	11*	12	14		8†								2
1	2	3	4	5	6	7		9	10†	11*	12	14		8								3
1	2	3	4	5	6	7*		9		11	12	10		8								4
	2	3	4	5	6	7		9	10	11			1	8								5
1	2	3		5	6	7	8	9	10	11					4							6
1	2	3	4†	5	6	7	8	9	10	11*					12	14						7
1	2	3		5	6	7	8*	9	10	11					4	12						8
1	2	3		5		7*	8	9	10	11				6	4	12						9
1		3	6				8	9	10	11				5	4	7	2					10
1	2	3		5	6		8	9	10	11					4	7*		12				11
1	2*	3		5	6	9	8		10†	11	12			7	4	14						12
1	2	3		5	6	9	8		10					7	4	11						13
1	2	3		5	6	9	8		10					7		11		4				14
1	2	3	7	5†	6	9	8		10					12	4	11*		14				15
1	2	3	4		6†	7*	8	9	10		12			11			5	14				16
1	2	3	4				8	9	10		7			6			5	11				17
1	2	11	4	5	3		8	9	10					7	6							18
1	2	3	4	5			8*	9	10					7	6	11		12				19
1		3	2		6	7		9	10					4	5	11		8				20
1		3	2	5		7		9	10					6*	4	11		12	8			21
1		3	2	5		7	8	9						6		11		4				22
1	2	3	4	5		7			10		11			6	9			8				23
1	2	3	4	5		7*	8		10					6	9			11	12			24
1	2		4	5			8		10		3			6	9			7	11			25
	2		4			7	8		10		3*	9	1	5		12			6	11		26
	2					7	8		10		3	12	1	4		9*	5	10	6	11		27
1	2	3	4	5		7	8		10						6	9			12	11*		28
1	2	3	4	5		7	8		10						6	9				11		29
1	2	3	4	5		7	8		10						6	9				11		30
1	2	3	4	5		7	8*		10†					12	6	9			14	11		31
1	2	3	4	5		7			10					12	6†	9*		8	14	11		32
1	2		4	5		7*	8		10		3					9		12	6	11		33
1	2		4	5		7	8		10		3			6		9				11		34
1	2		4	5		7*	8		10		3			14	6	9†		12	11			35
1	2		4	5		7	8		10		3			6		9			11			36
	2*		4	5		7	8		10†		3		1	6		9		12	11	14		37
1	2					7	8		10		3*			5	6	9	12		4	11		38
1	2	3		5			8		10					4	6			11	7	9		39
1	2	3		5		7	8		10°				15	11	6			4*	9	12		40
1	2	3		5		7	8		10					4	6			11		9		41
1	2	3		5		7	8		10					4	6			11		9		42
38	38	33	28	35	17	35	34	18	40	12	10	3	4	22	29	24	5	9	13	15		
											4	6	2	5	1	2	1	10	3	2	1	
	1	1	1	2	9	12	9	10		2	1		4	1	8		1	2				

1995-96

1	Aug	19	(h)	Coventry C	W	3-0	Lee, Beardsley (pen), Ferdinand	36,485
2		22	(a)	Bolton W	W	3-1	Ferdinand 2, Lee	20,243
3		27	(a)	Sheffield W	W	2-0	Ginola, Beardsley	24,815
4		30	(h)	Middlesbrough	W	1-0	Ferdinand	36,483
5	Sep	9	(a)	Southampton	L	0-1		15,237
6		16	(h)	Manchester C	W	3-1	Beardsley (pen), Ferdinand 2	36,501
7		24	(h)	Chelsea	W	2-0	Ferdinand 2	36,225
8	Oct	1	(a)	Everton	W	3-1	Ferdinand, Lee (pen), Kitson	33,026
9		14	(a)	QPR	W	3-2	Gillespie 2, Ferdinand	18,254
10		21	(h)	Wimbledon	W	6-1	Howey, Ferdinand 3, Clark, Albert	36,434
11		29	(a)	Tottenham H	D	1-1	Ginola	32,257
12	Nov	4	(h)	Liverpool	W	2-1	Ferdinand, Watson	36,547
13		8	(h)	Blackburn R	W	1-0	Lee	36,463
14		18	(a)	Aston Villa	D	1-1	Ferdinand	39,167
15		25	(h)	Leeds U	W	2-1	Lee, Beardsley	36,572
16	Dec	3	(a)	Wimbledon	D	3-3	Ferdinand 2, Gillespie	18,002
17		9	(a)	Chelsea	L	0-1		31,098
18		16	(h)	Everton	W	1-0	Ferdinand	36,557
19		23	(h)	Nottingham F	W	3-1	Lee 2, Ginola	36,531
20		27	(a)	Manchester U	L	0-2		42,024
21	Jan	2	(h)	Arsenal	W	2-0	Ginola, Ferdinand	36,530
22		14	(a)	Coventry C	W	1-0	Watson	20,532
23		20	(h)	Bolton W	W	2-1	Kitson, Beardsley	36,543
24	Feb	3	(h)	Sheffield W	W	2-0	Ferdinand, Clark	36,567
25		10	(a)	Middlesbrough	W	2-1	Watson, Ferdinand	30,011
26		21	(a)	West Ham U	L	0-2		23,843
27		24	(a)	Manchester C	D	3-3	Albert 2, Asprilla	31,115
28	Mar	4	(h)	Manchester U	L	0-1		36,584
29		18	(h)	West Ham U	W	3-0	Albert, Asprilla, Ferdinand	36,331
30		23	(a)	Arsenal	L	0-2		38,271
31	Apr	3	(a)	Liverpool	L	3-4	Ferdinand, Ginola, Asprilla	40,702
32		6	(h)	QPR	W	2-1	Beardsley 2	36,583
33		8	(a)	Blackburn R	L	1-2	Batty	30,717
34		14	(h)	Aston Villa	W	1-0	Ferdinand	36,546
35		17	(h)	Southampton	W	1-0	Lee	36,554
36		29	(a)	Leeds U	W	1-0	Gillespie	38,562
37	May	2	(a)	Nottingham F	D	1-1	Beardsley	28,280
38		5	(h)	Tottenham H	D	1-1	Ferdinand	36,589

FINAL LEAGUE POSITION: 2nd in the F.A. Premiership

Appearances

Sub. Appearances

Goals

Hislop S	Barton W	Beresford J	Clark L	Peacock D	Howey S	Lee R	Beardsley P	Ferdinand L	Ginola D	Gillespie K	Fox R	Kitson P	Watson S	Sellars S	Albert P	Hottiger M	Srnicek P	Elliott R	Huckerby D	Asprilla F	Batty D	
1	2	3	4	5	6	7	8	9	10*	11	12											1
1	2	3	4	5	6	7	8	9	10	11												2
1	2	3	4	5	6	7	8	9	10	11												3
1	2	3	4	5	6	7	8	9	10	11												4
1	2	3	4	5	6	7		9	10	11	8*	12										5
1	2†	3°	4	5	6	7	8*	9	10	11	12		13	14								6
1	2*	3	4	5	6	7		9	10†	11	8		12	13								7
1	2	3	4	5	6	7		9	10†	8*		13	12	11								8
1	2	3	4	5	6	7	8	9	10*	11				12								9
1	2	3	4*	5	6†	7°	8	9	10	11				12	13	14						10
1	2	3		5	6	7	8	9	4	10			11									11
1	2	3		5	6	7	8	9	10	11*			4		12							12
1	2	3		5	6	7	8	9	10	11			4									13
1	2	3	12	5	6	7	8	9†	10	11			4*		13							14
1	2	3	4	5	6	7	8	9	10	11												15
1	2	3	4	5	6	7	8	9	10	11												16
1°	2	3	4	5	6	7	8	9	10	11							15					17
	2	3	4	5	6	7	8	9	10	11*					12		1					18
	2	12	4	5	6	7	8	9	10	11†			13		3*		1					19
	2	3	4†	5	6	7	8	9	10	11*		13	12				1					20
	2	12		5	6	7*	8	9	10		11†	13			3		1	4				21
	2	3	4	5		7	8	9	10				11		6		1					22
	2	3	4	5		7	8		10			9*	11		6		1		12			23
	2	3	4		6	7	8	9		11*			12	10	5		1					24
	2	3	4	5		7	8	9		11*				10	6		1			12		25
	2	3	10	5	6		8	9		11*			12		4		1			7		26
	2	3	11	5	6		8	9	10						4		1			7		27
	2	3			6	7	8	9	10						5		1			11	4	28
	2*	3			6	7	8	9	10				12		5		1			11	4	29
	2*	3			6	7	8	9	10				12		5		1			11	4	30
		3	12	6*		7	8	9	10				2		5		1			11	4	31
1		3	5			7*	8	9	10		12		2		6					11	4	32
1		3	5			7	8	9	10		12		2		6					11*	4	33
1		3*	5			7	8	9	10				2		6				12	11	4	34
1		12	5			7	8	9	10				2		6			3		11*	4	35
1	12	13	5			7	8	9			11*		2		6			3		10†	4	36
1		12	5			7	8	9	10*	11†			2		6			3		13	4	37
1		12	5			7	8†	9	10	11*			2		6			3		13	4	38
24	30	32	22	33	28	36	35	37	34	26	2	2	15	2	19		14	5		11	11	
	1	1	6	1							2	2	5	8	4	4	1	1	1	1	3	
		2			1	8	8	25	5	4		2	3		4					3	1	

1996-97

1	Aug	17	(a)	Everton	L	0-2		40,117
2		21	(h)	Wimbledon	W	2-0	Batty, Shearer	36,385
3		24	(h)	Sheffield W	L	1-2	Shearer (pen)	36,452
4	Sep	4	(a)	Sunderland	W	2-1	Beardsley, Ferdinand	20,943
5		7	(a)	Tottenham H	W	2-1	Ferdinand 2	32,594
6		14	(h)	Blackburn R	W	2-1	Shearer (pen), Ferdinand	36,424
7		21	(a)	Leeds U	W	1-0	Shearer	36,070
8		30	(h)	Aston Villa	W	4-3	Ferdinand 2, Shearer, Howey	36,400
9	Oct	12	(a)	Derby Co	W	1-0	Shearer	18,092
10		20	(h)	Manchester U	W	5-0	Peacock, Ginola, Ferdinand, Shearer, Albert	36,579
11		26	(a)	Leicester C	L	0-2		21,134
12	Nov	3	(h)	Middlesbrough	W	3-1	Beardsley 2 (1 pen), Lee	36,577
13		16	(h)	West Ham U	D	1-1	Beardsley	36,552
14		23	(a)	Chelsea	D	1-1	Shearer	29,056
15		30	(h)	Arsenal	L	1-2	Shearer	36,565
16	Dec	9	(a)	Nottingham F	D	0-0		25,762
17		17	(a)	Coventry C	L	1-2	Shearer	22,092
18		23	(h)	Liverpool	D	1-1	Shearer	36,570
19		26	(a)	Blackburn R	L	0-1		30,398
20		28	(h)	Tottenham H	W	7-1	Shearer 2, Ferdinand 2, Lee 2, Albert	36,308
21	Jan	1	(h)	Leeds U	W	3-0	Shearer 2, Ferdinand	36,489
22		11	(a)	Aston Villa	D	2-2	Shearer, Clark	39,339
23		18	(a)	Southampton	D	2-2	Ferdinand, Clark	15,251
24		29	(h)	Everton	W	4-1	Ferdinand, Lee, Shearer (pen), Elliott	36,143
25	Feb	2	(h)	Leicester C	W	4-3	Elliott, Shearer 3	36,396
26		22	(a)	Middlesbrough	W	1-0	Ferdinand	30,063
27	Mar	1	(h)	Southampton	L	0-1		36,446
28		10	(a)	Liverpool	L	3-4	Gillespie, Asprilla, Barton	40,751
29		15	(h)	Coventry C	W	4-0	Watson, Lee, Beardsley (pen), Elliott	36,571
30		23	(a)	Wimbledon	D	1-1	Asprilla	23,343
31	Apr	5	(h)	Sunderland	D	1-1	Shearer	36,582
32		13	(a)	Sheffield W	D	1-1	Elliott	33,798
33		16	(h)	Chelsea	W	3-1	Shearer 2, Asprilla	36,320
34		19	(h)	Derby Co	W	3-1	Elliott, Ferdinand, Shearer	36,550
35	May	3	(a)	Arsenal	W	1-0	Elliott	38,179
36		6	(a)	West Ham U	D	0-0		24,617
37		8	(a)	Manchester U	D	0-0		55,236
38		11	(h)	Nottingham F	W	5-0	Asprilla, Ferdinand 2, Shearer, Elliott	36,544

FINAL LEAGUE POSITION: 2nd in the F.A. Premiership

Appearances

Sub. Appearances

Goals

76

Hislop S	Watson S	Beresford J	Batty D	Howey S	Albert P	Lee R	Gillespie K	Shearer A	Ferdinand L	Ginola D	Beardsley P	Elliott R	Asprilla F	Clark L	Srnicek P	Peacock D	Barton W	Kitson P	Crawford J	No.
1	2	3	4	5	6	7	8	9	10	11*	12									1
	2		4	5	6	7		9	10	11		3	8*	12	1					2
	2		4	5	6	7†	12	9	10	11		3	8*	13	1					3
	2		4		6	7		9	10*	11	8	3		12	1	5				4
	2			6		7		9	10	11	8	3		4	1	5				5
	2	3	4		6	7*	12	9	10°	11	8†		14	13	1	5				6
	2	3	4		6	7	12	9		11*	8†		10	13	1	5				7
	2	3	4		6	7	8	9	10	11*			12		1	5				8
	2	3	4		6	7	11	9	10		8				1	5				9
	2†	3	4		6	7*		9	10	11	8			12	1	5	13			10
	2†	3	4		6	7		9		11	8		12	10*	1	5		13		11
			4		6	7	2*	9		11	8	3	10		1	5	12			12
	12	13	4		6	7	2*	9°		11	8	3†	10	14	1	5				13
	12		4		6	7	2	9		11*	8	3	10†	13	1	5				14
	12		4		6	7*	2	9		11	8	3	10†		1	5		13		15
	2				6	7	4	9	10	11	8	3			1	5				16
	2				6	7	4	9	10	11	8	3			1	5				17
	2				6	7	4†	9	10°	11*	8	3		12	1	5	13	14		18
	2		4		6	7	11	9	10		8	3			1	5				19
1	2	3	4		6	7	11*	9	10		8			12		5				20
1	2	3	4		6	7		9	10		8			11		5				21
1	2	3	4		6		7	9			8	11		10		5				22
1		3	4		12	7*		9	10		8	11		5		5	2			23
1	2		4		6	7	11†	9	10		8*	3	12			5	13			24
1	2		4		6	7	11*	9	10	12		3	8†	13		5				25
1	4				6	7	8	9	10			3		11		5	2			26
1	4				6	7	11		10*	12	13	3	9	8†		5	2			27
1	2		4		6	7			13°	12	8†	3	9	10*		5	11	14		28
1	2		4		6	7†	12			11°	8	3	9*	13		5	10	14		29
1	2		4		6	7	8			11		3	9			5	10			30
1	6		4			7*	8	9	10†	11		3	13	12		5	2			31
1	6	3	4			7	8	9*	10			11	12			5	2			32
1	6	3	4			7	12†	9	10°	13		11	8*	14		5	2			33
1	6	3	4			7	12	9	10			11	8*			5	2			34
	6	3	4			7†	12	9	10			11	8*	13	1	5	2			35
	2	3	4		6		12	9				11	10*	7	1	5	8			36
	2	3	4		6	7		9	10*			11	12		1	5	8			37
	2	3	4†		6*		12	9	10		13	11	7°	14	1	5	8			38
16	33	18	32	8	27	32	23	31	30	20	22	29	17	9	22	35	14			
	3	1			1	9		1	4	3		7	16				4	3	2	
	1		1	1	2	5	1	25	16	1	5	7	4	2			1	1		

1997-98

1	Aug	9	(h)	Sheffield W	W	2-1	Asprilla 2	36,711
2		23	(h)	Aston Villa	W	1-0	Beresford	36,783
3	Sep	13	(h)	Wimbledon	L	1-3	Barton	36,692
4		20	(a)	West Ham U	W	1-0	Barnes	25,884
5		24	(h)	Everton	W	1-0	Lee	36,705
6		27	(a)	Chelsea	L	0-1		31,050
7	Oct	4	(h)	Tottenham H	W	1-0	Barton	36,708
8		18	(a)	Leeds U	L	1-4	Gillespie	39,865
9		25	(h)	Blackburn R	D	1-1	Gillespie	36,716
10	Nov	1	(h)	Leicester C	D	3-3	Barnes (pen), Tomasson, Beresford	36,754
11		8	(a)	Coventry C	D	2-2	Barnes, Lee	22,670
12		22	(h)	Southampton	W	2-1	Barnes 2	36,769
13		29	(a)	Crystal Palace	W	2-1	Ketsbaia, Tomasson	26,085
14	Dec	1	(a)	Bolton W	L	0-1		24,494
15		6	(h)	Arsenal	L	0-1		36,751
16		13	(a)	Barnsley	D	2-2	Gillespie 2	18,694
17		17	(h)	Derby Co	D	0-0		36,289
18		21	(h)	Manchester U	L	0-1		36,763
19		26	(a)	Derby Co	L	0-1		30,232
20		28	(h)	Liverpool	L	1-2	Watson	36,702
21	Jan	10	(a)	Sheffield W	L	1-2	Tomasson	29,446
22		17	(h)	Bolton W	W	2-1	Barnes, Ketsbaia	36,767
23		20	(a)	Liverpool	L	0-1		42,791
24	Feb	1	(a)	Aston Villa	W	1-0	Batty	38,266
25		7	(h)	West Ham U	L	0-1		36,736
26		22	(h)	Leeds U	D	1-1	Ketsbaia	36,511
27		28	(a)	Everton	D	0-0		37,972
28	Mar	14	(h)	Coventry C	D	0-0		36,762
29		18	(h)	Crystal Palace	L	1-2	Shearer	36,565
30		28	(a)	Southampton	L	1-2	Lee	15,251
31		31	(a)	Wimbledon	D	0-0		15,478
32	Apr	11	(a)	Arsenal	L	1-3	Barton	38,102
33		13	(h)	Barnsley	W	2-1	Andersson, Shearer	36,534
34		18	(a)	Manchester U	D	1-1	Andersson	55,194
35		25	(a)	Tottenham H	L	0-2		35,847
36		29	(a)	Leicester C	D	0-0		21,699
37	May	2	(h)	Chelsea	W	3-1	Dabizas, Lee, Speed	36,710
38		10	(a)	Blackburn R	L	0-1		29,300

FINAL LEAGUE POSITION: 13th in the F.A. Premiership

Appearances

Sub. Appearances

Goals

#	Given S	Watson S	Beresford J	Albert P	Pistone A	Pearce S	Lee R	Batty D	Asprilla F	Ketsbaia T	Tomasson J	Rush I	Gillespie K	Barton W	Barnes J	Peacock D	Howey S	Srnicek P	Damilton D	Hislop S	Hughes A	Shearer A	Griffin A	Andersson A	Speed G	Dabizas N
1	1	2	3	4	5	6	7	8	9	10	11															
2	1	2	3	4	5	6	7	8		11†	12	9*	10	13												
3	1	2	3	4	5		7		12	13	11	9	8*	6†	10											
4	1	2	3	6			7	8	9		11		4	10*	5	12										
5	1	2	12	6	3		7*	4	9	11†	13	8°	14	10	5											
6	1	2	3°	4	5			8	12	11*	9	13	7	10†	6	14										
7	1	2	3					4		7	11	9	8	10	5	6										
8	1	4	3				7	8		11*	12	9	13	2	10†	5	6									
9		2	3	6			12	4		11		9	8†		10	5	13	1	7*							
10	1	2	3	4			7	8		11	9*	12	10	5	6†				13							
11	1	2	3	4	5		7	8*	9		11	12	10	6												
12		2		6	3		7	4		8	9		11		10	5				1						
13		2		5	3	12	4			8	9		11	10*	6				7	1						
14		2		5	3	7	4			9	10		11	12	6				8*	1						
15		2	12	5	3	7	4	9*		13	8†		11	10	6					1						
16		2		4	5	3	7	8	9*		12		11	10	6					1						
17		2		6	5	3		4	9*	8	11	12	7		10					1						
18		2	11*	4†	3	6		8	9	12			7	13	10	5				1						
19		2	11		3	6		4	12	13	10†	9*	7	14			5°		8	1						
20		4	3		5	6	7	8	9		11	2*	10		12					1						
21		6	11		4				12	9	13		7	2*	10	5			8†	1	3					
22		4	11		3	6	7		12	9*		8	2	10†	5					1			13			
23		4	11*		3	6	7		12	9		8	2	10†						1		5	13			
24		2	3	4		6	7	8	12		11					5				1		9		10*		
25	1			2		6	7	4	12		8					5						9	3*	10	11	
26	1		12	3		6	7	4	13		8*					5			2†			9		10	11	
27	1		6		3		7	4	12		8*	2				5						9		10	11	
28	1		6*	2	3†		7	4	8		12					5						9		10†	11	13
29	1		3					4	8*	12	7	2	13	14		5°						9		10†	11	6
30	1		3		6	7†	8		12	8	11*	10			13						2	9			4	
31	1	2		4		3		8	12	13		5†	7									9	6*		11	10
32	1		6		3		4	12	7	10†	8*											9	2	13	11	5
33	1	12	6		3		7	4	13		8†		2									9		10*	11	5
34	1		4		3	6	7	8	12		2											9		10*	11	5
35	1	2	4*		3	6		8	13		12†		7									9		10	11	5
36	1				3	6	7	8	10		2						5					9			11	4
37	1	12			3	6	7°	8			2		13				5*		14			9		10†	11	4
38	1	4			6	3		8	7*		10†		2		12							9	2	13	11	5
	24	27	17	21	28	25	26	32	8	16	17	6	25	17	22	19	11	1	7	13	4	15	4	10	13	10
		2	1	2		2		2	15	6	4	4	6	4	1	3		5			2		2		1	
		1	2				4	1	2	3	3		4	3	6				2		2		1	1		

79

1998-99

1	Aug	15	(h)	Charlton Athletic	D	0-0		36,719
2		22	(a)	Chelsea	D	1-1	Andersson	34,795
3		30	(h)	Liverpool	L	1-4	Guivarc'h	36,740
4	Sep	9	(a)	Aston Villa	L	0-1		39,241
5		12	(h)	Southampton	W	4-0	Shearer 2 (1 pen), Marshall (og), Ketsbaia	36,454
6		19	(a)	Coventry City	W	5-1	Dabizas, Shearer 2, Speed, Glass	22,639
7		26	(h)	Nottingham Forest	W	2-0	Shearer 2 (1 pen)	36,760
8	Oct	4	(a)	Arsenal	L	0-3		38,102
9		17	(h)	Derby County	W	2-1	Dabizas, Glass	36,750
10		24	(a)	Tottenham Hotspur	L	0-2		36,047
11		31	(h)	West Ham United	L	0-3		36,744
12	Nov	8	(a)	Manchester United	D	0-0		55,174
13		14	(h)	Sheffield Wednesd	D	1-1	Dalglish	36,698
14		23	(a)	Everton	L	0-1		30,357
15		28	(h)	Wimbledon	W	3-1	Solano, Ferguson 2	36,623
16	Dec	6	(a)	Middlesbrough	D	2-2	Charvet, Dabizas	34,629
17		12	(a)	Blackburn Rovers	D	0-0		27,569
18		19	(h)	Leicester City	W	1-0	Glass	36,718
19		26	(h)	Leeds United	L	0-3		36,759
20		28	(a)	Liverpool	L	2-4	Solano, Andersson	44,605
21	Jan	9	(h)	Chelsea	L	0-1		36,711
22		17	(a)	Charlton Athletic	D	2-2	Ketsbaia, Solano	20,043
23		30	(h)	Aston Villa	W	2-1	Shearer, Ketsbaia	36,766
24	Feb	6	(a)	Leeds United	W	1-0	Solano	40,202
25		17	(h)	Coventry City	W	4-1	Shearer 2, Speed, Saha	36,352
26		20	(a)	Southampton	L	1-2	Hamann	15,244
27		28	(h)	Arsenal	D	1-1	Hamann	36,708
28	Mar	10	(a)	Nottingham Forest	W	2-1	Shearer (pen), Hamann	22,852
29		13	(h)	Manchester United	L	1-2	Solano	36,776
30		20	(a)	West Ham United	L	0-2		25,997
31	Apr	3	(a)	Derby County	W	4-3	Speed 2, Ketsbaia, Solano	32,039
32		5	(h)	Tottenham Hotspur	D	1-1	Ketsbaia	36,655
33		17	(h)	Everton	L	1-3	Shearer (pen)	36,775
34		21	(a)	Sheffield Wednesd	D	1-1	Shearer (pen)	21,545
35		24	(a)	Wimbledon	D	1-1	Shearer	21,325
36	May	1	(h)	Middlesbrough	D	1-1	Shearer (pen)	36,784
37		8	(a)	Leicester City	L	0-2		21,125
38		16	(h)	Blackburn Rovers	D	1-1	Hamann	36,623

FINAL LEAGUE POSITION: 13th in the F.A. Premiership

Appearances

Sub. Appearances

Goals

Given SJ	Watson SC	Pearce S	Charvet LJ	Pistone A	Dabizas N	Lee RM	Hamann D	Shearer A	Andersson AC	Speed GA	Barnes J	Ketsbaia T	Barton WD	Albert P	Solano NA	Serrant C	Guivarc'h S	Glass S	Gillespie KR	Dalglish P	Batty D	Griffin A	Hughes AW	Georgiades G	Brady G	Howey SN	Ferguson D	Harper SA	Domi D	Saha L	Maric S	McClen JD	Beharall DA	
1	2	3	4	5	6*	7	8	9	10°	11	12†	13	14																					1
1	2	3	4	5*	6	7	8	9	10†	11				12	13																			2
1	2*	6	4		12	7	8°	9		11				13	5		3†	10	14															3
1	2	3	6			7		9	10*	11				13	5		4†	12	8															4
1	2	3	6			7		9	10†	11*				8	13	5		4	12															5
1	2	3	6	5			8	9		12		13		4*		10°	11	7†	14															6
1	2*	3	6	5			8	9		4		10†		12	7°			11*					14	13										7
1		3	6	5			8	9	10†			13			7			11*	12		4	2												8
1		3	6	5			8	9		12		13			7*			11	10†		4	2												9
1		6	5				8	9	13			7		3	12			11*	10†		4	2												10
1		3	6	14	5			9		8		12			7†			11*	13	10°	4	2												11
1		2		6		8*	9			12					11				10	4	3	5	7											12
1		6			4	8*	9†	14	11			2				12			7	10	13	3°	5											13
1		6		5	8	12		9	11			2*	13		3†			7	10°	4			14											14
1°	2				8		10	4		3		13			11*	7					6			5	9	12								15
	2		12	4			10°	8		3*		7†	13		11	14					6			5	9	1								16
	2		12		8		10†	4	13	3		7			11°						6*	14		5	9	1								17
1	2		6	4		12	9	8	10*	3					11							7	5											18
1	2		6	4			9	8	13	3†					11						12	7*	5	10										19
1	3	2		12		8	9	13	4						7*			11°			6	14	5	10†										20
1		2			12	8	9	10†	4						7*			11			6		5			3	13							21
		13	6				9		4	10†	2				7°				14		12	11	8*	5		1	3							22
1		6			8	9	13	4	10*	2					7†			11			12	5			3									23
1		6			8		12	4	10	2					7			11†		3		13	5			9*								24
1	2		6		8	9		4†	13	12					7			11°		14		5		3	10*									25
1	2		6	12	8	9		4	10						7*			11			5		3											26
1	2		6	13	8	9		4	12						7†			11*			5		3	10										27
1		6	13	12	8	9		4†	14	2					11						5*		3	10°	7									28
1		6	5	14	8	9		4	10†	2°					7			11*					3	13	12									29
1		6	5	13		9		4		12					7					2	11*		3	10	8†									30
1		6	5	10				11	9			7†			2					4		12	3	13	8*									31
1		6	5					4	9	12		7							3*	2	13		11	14	10°	8†								32
1				4	8	9		11	10*	3		13								2	6				12	7†		5						33
		6	7†	8	9*	4		10	3	13										2	5	12				1		11						34
1		6		8	9	10	4			7										2				3				11	5					35
		6	7	8	9	4		12	2	13										10†	1	3		11*				5						36
		6	4	8	9	11		13	2	7†		12								10*	1	3						5						37
		6	4*	8			11	9†	3	7		12								2	5			1		13	10							38
31	7	12	30	2	25	20	22	29	11	34		14	17	3	24	3	2	18	5	6	6	14	12	7	3	14	7	7	14	5	9	1	4	
	1		1	5	6	1	1		4	4	1	12	7	3	5	1	2	4	2	5	2		2	3	6			1		6	1			
		1		3		4	14	2	4			5			6		1	3		1				2					1					

81

1999-2000

1	Aug	7	(h)	Aston Villa	L	0-1		36,376
2		9	(a)	Tottenham Hotspur	L	1-3	Solano	28,701
3		15	(a)	Southampton	L	2-4	Shearer (pen), Speed	15,030
4		21	(h)	Wimbledon	D	3-3	Speed, Domi, Solano (pen)	35,809
5		25	(h)	Sunderland	L	1-2	Dyer	36,420
6		30	(a)	Manchester United	L	1-5	Berg (og)	55,190
7	Sep	11	(a)	Chelsea	L	0-1		35,081
8		19	(h)	Sheffield Wednesd	W	8-0	Hughes, Shearer 5 (2 pens), Dyer, Speed	36,619
9		25	(a)	Leeds United	L	2-3	Shearer 2	40,192
10	Oct	3	(h)	Middlesbrough	W	2-1	Shearer 2	36,421
11		16	(a)	Coventry City	L	1-4	Domi	23,022
12		25	(h)	Derby County	W	2-0	Eranio (og), Shearer	35,614
13		30	(a)	Arsenal	D	0-0		38,106
14	Nov	7	(h)	Everton	D	1-1	Shearer	36,164
15		20	(a)	Watford	D	1-1	Dabizas	19,539
16		28	(h)	Tottenham Hotspur	W	2-1	Glass, Dabizas	36,454
17	Dec	4	(a)	Aston Villa	W	1-0	Ferguson	34,531
18		18	(a)	Bradford City	L	0-2		18,276
19		26	(h)	Liverpool	D	2-2	Shearer, Ferguson	36,445
20		28	(a)	Leicester City	W	2-1	Ferguson, Shearer	21,225
21	Jan	3	(h)	West Ham United	D	2-2	Dabizas, Speed	36,314
22		16	(h)	Southampton	W	5-0	Ferguson 2, Solano, Dryden (og), Monk (og)	35,623
23		22	(a)	Wimbledon	L	0-2		22,118
24	Feb	5	(a)	Sunderland	D	2-2	Domi, Helder	42,079
25		12	(h)	Manchester United	W	3-0	Ferguson, Shearer 2	36,470
26		26	(a)	Sheffield Wednesd	W	2-0	Gallacher, Shearer	29,212
27	Mar	4	(h)	Chelsea	L	0-1		36,448
28		11	(h)	Watford	W	1-0	Gallacher	36,433
29		19	(a)	Everton	W	2-0	Hughes, Dyer	32,512
30		25	(a)	Liverpool	L	1-2	Shearer	44,743
31	Apr	1	(h)	Bradford City	W	2-0	Speed, Shearer	36,572
32		12	(a)	West Ham United	L	1-2	Speed	25,817
33		15	(h)	Leicester City	L	0-2		36,426
34		23	(h)	Leeds United	D	2-2	Shearer 2	36,448
35		29	(h)	Coventry City	W	2-0	Shearer (pen), Gavilan	36,408
36	May	2	(a)	Middlesbrough	D	2-2	Speed, Pistone	34,744
37		6	(a)	Derby County	D	0-0		32,724
38		14	(h)	Arsenal	W	4-2	Speed 2, Shearer, Griffin	36,450

FINAL LEAGUE POSITION: 11th in the F.A. Premiership

Appearances

Sub. Appearances

Goals

Harper SA	Barton WD	Domi D	Dumas F	Goma A	Marcelino	Solano NA	Speed GA	Shearer A	Ketsbaia T	Serrant C	Dyer KC	Robinson PD	Maric S	Hughes AW	Karelse J	McClen JD	Beharall D	Ferguson D	Wright TJ	Dabizas N	Lee RM	Glass S	Charvet LJ	Gallacher KW	Given SJJ	Pistone A	Helder RC	Fumaca	Gavilan ZDA	Howey SN	Griffin A	
1	2	3	4	5	6*	7†	8	9	10	11°	12	13	14																			1
1	2	3	4*	5		11	8	9	10		7	12	13	6†																		2
	2	3		5		7	4	9	10	11*	8	13	12†	6	1																	3
	2	3		5*	6	7	11		10†		4	9			1	8	12	13														4
	2	3		5		7	4	13			10	9†	11*			8		12	1	6												5
	2			5		11†	8	9			7	14		3		12	13	10*	1	6	4°											6
	2	3		5		11*	8	9			7	13	12	14				10°	1	6	4†											7
1	2	3°		5		11	8	9	10†		7*	13		6		14					4	12										8
1	2	3		5	6	11	4	9	10*		7	13				8†							12									9
1	2	3		5		11†	8	9			7	12								6	4		13	10*								10
	2	3				11	8	9			7			5						6	4			10	1							11
	2*			5		11	8	9			7°		13	12				14		6	4			10†	1	3						12
		3	4	5		7*	11	9							1			12		6		8		10		2						13
1		3		5		7	11	9				12				10*				6	4			8		2						14
1			4	5			11	9	12			10†	2							6	7	13		8*		3						15
1						7*		9	10°			12	3		13			14		6	4		11	2					5	8†		16
1	12	2				7*	11	9	10†			8°	14					13		6	4					3	5					17
1	2					7*	11	9	10†			13	6					10			4°	14		8†		3	5	12				18
1	2					7°	8	9	13			11†		5				10*		6	4		14	12		3						19
1	2			5		7	11	9										10		6	4			8		3						20
1	2			5		7	11	9	14									10*		6	4°		13	8†		3		12				21
1	2°	14		5		7†	11	9	13			4		12				10		6				8*		3						22
1	2	12		5		7	11	9				4						10		6				8*		3						23
1	2	11†					8	9			7			12				10		6	4°		14			3*	5			13		24
1	2	13					11	9	14			7°		3				10†		6	4			8*			5	12				25
	2	13					11	9	14			7		3				10†		6	4			8*	1	5°		12				26
	2	11*				13	8	9	12			7		3				10		6	4†			13	1					5		27
	2	12				7	11	9						3*				10		6	4			8	1					5		28
	2	13				7†	11	9				12		3				10		6	4			8*	1					5		29
	2	12		4*			11	9				7		3				10		6	8†		13		1					5		30
1	2	11		6			8	9	12			7*		3				10			4					5						31
	2	11		5		7	8	9	13			10*		3						6†	4				1						12	32
	2	11		5		7*	8	9				10†	12	3°							4				1				14	13	6	33
	2	11			12			9				10†	14	3						6	8				1	4*	13	7°	5			34
	2	11*					8	9	14			10		5		12				6	4†				1	3			7°		13	35
	2					7°	11	9	10*			8†	14	5		13				6	4				1	3				12		36
	2	12				7†	11	9	10°			8		5						6	4		13		1	3*		14				37
	2					7*	11	9	10°			8	13			12				6	4†		14		1					5	3	38
18	33	19	6	14	10	29	36	36	11	2	27	2	3	22	3	3		17	3	29	30	1	1	15	14	15	8	1	2	7	1	
	1	8		1	1		1			10		3	9	10	5		6	2	6					6	1	5		4	4	2	2	
		3					3	9	23			3			2			6		3			1		2		1	1		1		1	

83

2000-2001

1	Aug	20	(a)	Manchester United	L	0-2		67,477
2		23	(h)	Derby County	W	3-2	Cort, Cordone, Glass	51,327
3		26	(h)	Tottenham Hotspur	W	2-0	Speed, Cordone	51,503
4	Sep	6	(a)	Coventry City	W	2-0	Shearer (pen), Gallacher	22,102
5		9	(h)	Chelsea	D	0-0		51,687
6		16	(a)	Southampton	L	0-2		15,221
7		23	(h)	Charlton Athletic	L	0-1		50,768
8		30	(a)	Manchester City	W	1-0	Shearer	34,497
9	Oct	16	(a)	Middlesbrough	W	3-1	Shearer, Goma, Dyer	31,436
10		21	(h)	Everton	L	0-1		51,625
11		28	(a)	West Ham United	L	0-1		26,044
12	Nov	4	(h)	Ipswich Town	W	2-1	Shearer 2 (1 pen)	50,922
13		11	(a)	Leicester City	D	1-1	Speed	21,406
14		18	(h)	Sunderland	L	1-2	Speed	52,030
15		26	(h)	Liverpool	W	2-1	Solano, Dyer	51,949
16	Dec	2	(a)	Aston Villa	D	1-1	Solano	34,255
17		9	(a)	Arsenal	L	0-5		38,052
18		16	(h)	Bradford City	W	2-1	Speed, Dyer	50,470
19		23	(a)	Derby County	L	0-2		29,978
20		26	(h)	Leeds United	W	2-1	Solano, Acuna	52,118
21		30	(h)	Manchester United	D	1-1	Glass	52,134
22	Jan	2	(a)	Tottenham Hotspur	L	2-4	Solano, Dyer (pen)	34,323
23		13	(h)	Coventry City	W	3-1	Speed, Ameobi, Dyer	50,159
24		20	(a)	Leeds United	W	3-1	Solano (pen), Acuna, Ameobi	40,005
25		31	(a)	Chelsea	L	1-3	Bassedas	35,108
26	Feb	11	(a)	Charlton Athletic	L	0-2		20,043
27		24	(h)	Manchester City	L	0-1		51,981
28	Mar	3	(a)	Everton	D	1-1	Unsworth (og)	35,779
29		17	(h)	Middlesbrough	L	1-2	Cort	51,751
30		31	(a)	Bradford City	D	2-2	Cort, Acuna	20,160
31	Apr	14	(a)	Ipswich Town	L	0-1		24,026
32		16	(h)	West Ham United	W	2-1	Cort, Solano (pen)	51,107
33		21	(a)	Sunderland	D	1-1	O'Brien	47,213
34		28	(h)	Leicester City	W	1-0	Cort	50,501
35	May	1	(h)	Southampton	D	1-1	Gallacher	50,439
36		5	(a)	Liverpool	L	0-3		44,363
37		15	(h)	Arsenal	D	0-0		50,729
38		19	(h)	Aston Villa	W	3-0	Glass, Cort, Delaney (og)	51,306

FINAL LEAGUE POSITION: 11th in the F.A. Premiership

Appearances

Sub. Appearances

Goals

Given SJ	Barton WD	Hughes AW	Goma A	Marcelino	Dabizas N	Lee RM	Cordone CD	Shearer A	Cort CER	Speed GA	Dyer KC	Solano NA	Domi D	Charvet LJ	Glass S	Coppinger J	Griffin A	Kerr B	Gallacher KW	Gavilan D	Ameobi F	Lua-Lua LT	Caldwell S	Acuna DCW	Bassedas CG	Harper SA	Quinn WR	O'Brien AJ	
1	2	3	4*	5	6	7†	8	9	10	11	12	13																	1
1	2	5	12	6*			8	9	10°	11	4	7†	3	13	14														2
1	2	6	5				10†	9		8	4	7	3		11*	12	13												3
1		6	5		4		10°	9		8		7	3*	2	11†	12	13		14										4
1	3	6	5				10	9		11	4	7†		2							8*	12	13						5
1		6	5				10	9		11	4	7	3*	2		12					8†		13						6
1		6	5			14	8*	9	10	11	4	7†	13	2°		3					12								7
1		6			4		10†	9		11	7*	13	3	5	2°	8						12		14					8
1		6	5		4		10*	9	8	11		7	3	2		12													9
1	2*	6	5		4		10†	9	8	11		7	3			12	13												10
1		6	5		4†	13		9		11		7	3	2		12					8			10*					11
1		6	5		4		10*	9		11		7	3		2†							14	12	8°	13				12
1		6	5		4*	12		9		11		7	3	2							8				10				13
1	12	6			4			9		11		7	3	2							8*		13	5	10†				14
1	3	5			4			9	8	11		7	6	2								12		10*					15
1	3	6°	5*		4†			9	10	11		7	13	2								14	12	8					16
1	3	6			4°	14		9*		11		12	13	2†									10	5	8				17
1	3	6	5		4			9	8	11		7		2								12		10*					18
1*	3	6	5			7°	14	9	10			13	2										4†	8	11	12			19
	3	6	5		4		10					7		2							9			8	11	1			20
	3	6	5		13	4	10					7				12	2				9*	14		8†	11°	1			21
	3	6	5		4		10					7				12	2*				9†	13		8	11	1			22
	2	6	5		4		10					7				12					9			8	11*	1		3	23
1	2	6	5	13	4†					11		7								10°	9*	14		8	12			3	24
1	2	6	5	12	4		10†					7									9*	13		8	11			3	25
1	2	6	5		4†	11	10					7°				14					9	13		8*	12			3	26
1	12	6	5					9			4	7				14	2			11†	10°	13		8*				3	27
1		6			4	12		9				7*				14	2		13		10°	5		8	11†			3	28
1	2†	6			4	13	10			11		7*				12				14	9°	5		8*				3	29
1	2	6			4		10			11		7*				12					9			8†	13		3	5	30
1	2	6			4†		10			11		7				13					9*	12		8			3	5	31
1	2*	6			4†			9		11		7									10°	14	12	13	8		3	5	32
1	2	6				14		9			4	7†							13		10*	12		8°	11		3	5	33
1	2	6						9			4	7									10*	12	13	8	11†		3	5	34
1	2	13			6			9			4	7									10†	12		8	11*		3	5	35
1	2		4		6			9†		11		7									10°	14	13	8*	12		3	5	36
1	2		3		6			9			4	7				11					10*	12		8				5	37
1	2		3		6			9			4	7°			11†						10*	13	12	8			14	5	38
34	27	34	18	5	9	21	12	19	13	35	25	31	11	6	5	14	12	12	3	5	23	17	4	14	9				
	2	1	1	1	1		9		1	2	3	1		9	1	5	1	7	1	8	18	4	3	5	1	1			
			1				2	5	6	5	5	6			3					2	2			3	1			1	

2001-2002

1	Aug	19	(a)	Chelsea	D	1-1	Acuna	40,124
2		26	(h)	Sunderland	D	1-1	Bellamy	52,021
3	Sep	8	(a)	Middlesbrough	W	4-1	Shearer 2 (1 pen), Dabizas, Robert	30,004
4		15	(h)	Manchester United	W	4-3	Robert, Lee, Dabizas, Brown (og)	52,056
5		23	(a)	West Ham United	L	0-3		28,840
6		26	(h)	Leicester City	W	1-0	Solano	49,185
7		30	(h)	Liverpool	L	0-2		52,095
8	Oct	13	(a)	Bolton Wanderers	W	4-0	Solano, Robert, Shearer, Bellamy	25,631
9		21	(h)	Tottenham Hotspur	L	0-2		50,593
10		27	(a)	Everton	W	3-1	Bellamy, Solano, Acuna	37,524
11	Nov	3	(h)	Aston Villa	W	3-0	Bellamy 2, Shearer	51,057
12		17	(a)	Fulham	L	1-3	Speed	21,159
13		24	(h)	Derby County	W	1-0	Shearer (pen)	50,070
14	Dec	1	(a)	Charlton Athletic	D	1-1	Speed	24,151
15		9	(a)	Ipswich Town	W	1-0	Solano	24,748
16		15	(h)	Blackburn Rovers	W	2-1	Bernard, Speed	50,064
17		18	(a)	Arsenal	W	3-1	O'Brien, Shearer (pen), Robert	38,012
18		22	(a)	Leeds United	W	4-3	Bellamy, Elliott, Shearer (pen), Solano	40,287
19		26	(h)	Middlesbrough	W	3-0	Shearer, Speed, Bernard	52,127
20		29	(h)	Chelsea	L	1-2	Shearer	52,123
21	Jan	2	(a)	Manchester United	L	1-3	Shearer	67,646
22		12	(h)	Leeds United	W	3-1	Duberry (og), Dyer, Bellamy	52,130
23		19	(a)	Leicester City	D	0-0		21,354
24		30	(a)	Tottenham Hotspur	W	3-1	Acuna, Shearer, Bellamy	35,798
25	Feb	2	(h)	Bolton Wanderers	W	3-2	Shearer 2, Bellamy	52,094
26		9	(h)	Southampton	W	3-1	Robert, Shearer 2 (1 pen)	51,857
27		24	(a)	Sunderland	W	1-0	Dabizas	48,290
28	Mar	2	(h)	Arsenal	L	0-2		52,067
29		6	(a)	Liverpool	L	0-3		44,204
30		16	(h)	Ipswich Town	D	2-2	Robert, Shearer	51,115
31		29	(h)	Everton	W	6-2	Shearer, Cort, O'Brien, Solano 2, Bernard	51,921
32	Apr	2	(a)	Aston Villa	D	1-1	Shearer	36,597
33		8	(h)	Fulham	D	1-1	Dyer	50,017
34		13	(a)	Derby County	W	3-2	Robert, Dyer, Lua-Lua	31,031
35		20	(h)	Charlton Athletic	W	3-0	Speed, Lua-Lua, Shearer	51,360
36		23	(a)	Blackburn Rovers	D	2-2	Shearer 2	26,712
37		27	(h)	West Ham United	W	3-1	Shearer, Lua-Lua, Robert	52,127
38	May	11	(a)	Southampton	L	1-3	Shearer	31,973

FINAL LEAGUE POSITION: 4th in the F.A. Premiership

Appearances

Sub. Appearances

Goals

Given SJJ	Barton WD	Elliott RJ	Lee RM	Hughes AW	Dabizas N	Bassedas CG	Acuna DCW	Ameobi F	Bellamy CD	Robert L	Griffin A	O'Brien AJ	Lua-Lua LT	Solano NA	Speed GA	Shearer A	Distin S	Bernard O	Dyer KC	McClen JD	Jenas JA	Cort CER	Match
1	2	3	4	5	6	7†	8*	9°	10	11	12	13	14										1
1	2	3†	4	5	6		13	9°	10	11		12		7	8*	14							2
1	2°	3	4	5	6		8	13	10†	11		12	14	7		9*							3
1	12	3	4*		6		8		10†	11	2	5		7		9	13						4
1	2†	3	4		6		8	13	10	11		5		7*		9	12						5
1		3	4		6		8	12	10	11	2	5		7		9*							6
1		3	4		6		8†	12	10	11	2	5		7*	13	9							7
1		3	4	2	6°		13	14	10†	11		5		7	8*	9	12						8
1			2*	6	14	8†	12		10	11		5	13	7°	4	9	3						9
1		3		2	6		8		10	11		5	12	7*	4	9							10
1		3	4	2	6				10	11*		5		7	8	9		12					11
1		3	4*	2	6°			12	10	11		5	14	7†	8	9	13						12
1		3	4	2	6				10	11*		5	12	7	8	9							13
1		3	4	2	6			12	10*	11†		5	13	7	8	9							14
1		3	4	2	6				10	11*		5		7†	8	9		13	12				15
1		3	4†	2			10*					5	13	7	8	9	6	11	12				16
1		3*		2	6				10	12		5	14	7†	8	9	13	11	4°				17
1		3		2	6†				10*	11°		5	13	7	8	9	12	14	4				18
1		3	13	2					10	11°		5	12	7*	8	9	6	14	4†				19
1		3†		2					10	11		5	13	7*	8	9	6	12	4				20
1		3	4	2	6			13	10*					7†	8	9	5	12	11				21
1		3		2	6				10	11		5*		7	8	9	12		4				22
1		3		2	6				10	11				7	8	9	5		4				23
1	11*			2	6		8		10	12		5		7		9	3		4				24
1				2	6		12		10	11		5		7	8	9	3		4*				25
1	12			2	6				10	11		5		7	8	9	3*		4†	13			26
1				2	6			12	10	11*		5		7	4	9	3		8				27
1				2†	6			10*		11		5	13	7	4	9	3		8	12			28
1				2	6			12		11		5		7	4*	9	3	13	8	10†			29
1				2	6		8	14		11		5	13	7†		9	3		12	4°	10*		30
1				2	6			12		11°		5	13	7		9	3	14	4*	8	10†		31
1				2	6			12		11†		5		7		9	3	13	4	8	10*		32
1		3		2	12					11		5*		7	8	9	6		4	13	10†		33
1				2	6					11		5†	14	7	8	9°	3	12	4	13	10*		34
1		3		2	12					11†		5*	10	7°	8	9	6	14	4	13			35
1		3†		2	6			13		11			10*	7	8	9	5	12	4				36
1				2	6					11		5*	10°	7	8	9	13	3	4†	12	14		37
1				2	6					11		10		7	8	9	5	3	4*	12			38
38	4	26	15	34	33	1	10	4	26	34	3	31	4	37	28	36	20	4	15	3	6	6	
	1	1	1	2	1	6	11	1	2	1	3		16	1	1	8	12	3		6	2		
		1	1		3		3		9	8		2	3	7	5	23		3	3			1	

2002-2003

1	Aug	19	(h)	West Ham United	W	4-0	Lua-Lua 2, Shearer, Solano	51,072
2		24	(a)	Manchester City	L	0-1		34,776
3	Sep	2	(a)	Liverpool	D	2-2	Speed, Shearer	43,241
4		11	(h)	Leeds United	L	0-2		51,730
5		14	(a)	Chelsea	L	0-3		39,746
6		21	(h)	Sunderland	W	2-0	Bellamy, Shearer	52,181
7		28	(a)	Birmingham City	W	2-0	Solano, Ameobi	29,072
8	Oct	5	(h)	West Bromwich Alb	W	2-1	Shearer 2	52,142
9		19	(a)	Blackburn Rovers	L	2-5	Shearer 2 (1 pen)	27,307
10		26	(h)	Charlton Athletic	W	2-1	Griffin, Robert	51,670
11	Nov	4	(h)	Middlesbrough	W	2-0	Ameobi, Caldwell	51,558
12		9	(a)	Arsenal	L	0-1		38,121
13		16	(h)	Southampton	W	2-1	Ameobi, Hughes	51,812
14		23	(a)	Manchester United	L	3-5	Bernard, Shearer, Bellamy	67,619
15	Dec	1	(h)	Everton	W	2-1	Shearer, Li Tie (og)	51,607
16		7	(a)	Aston Villa	W	1-0	Shearer	33,446
17		14	(a)	Southampton	D	1-1	Bellamy	32,061
18		21	(h)	Fulham	W	2-0	Solano, Bellamy	51,576
19		26	(a)	Bolton Wanderers	L	3-4	Shearer 2, Ameobi	27,314
20		29	(h)	Tottenham Hotspur	W	2-1	Speed, Shearer	52,145
21	Jan	1	(h)	Liverpool	W	1-0	Robert	52,147
22		11	(a)	West Ham United	D	2-2	Bellamy, Jenas	35,048
23		18	(h)	Manchester City	W	2-0	Shearer, Bellamy	52,152
24		22	(h)	Bolton Wanderers	W	1-0	Jenas	52,005
25		29	(a)	Tottenham Hotspur	W	1-0	Jenas	36,084
26	Feb	9	(h)	Arsenal	D	1-1	Robert	52,157
27		22	(a)	Leeds United	W	3-0	Dyer 2, Shearer	40,025
28	Mar	1	(h)	Chelsea	W	2-1	Hasselbaink (og), Bernard	52,157
29		5	(a)	Middlesbrough	L	0-1		34,814
30		15	(a)	Charlton Athletic	W	2-0	Shearer (pen), Solano	26,728
31		22	(h)	Blackburn Rovers	W	5-1	Solano, Robert, Jenas, Gresko (og), Bellamy	52,106
32	Apr	6	(a)	Everton	L	1-2	Robert	40,031
33		12	(h)	Manchester United	L	2-6	Jenas, Ameobi	52,164
34		19	(a)	Fulham	L	1-2	Shearer	17,900
35		21	(h)	Aston Villa	D	1-1	Solano	52,015
36		26	(a)	Sunderland	W	1-0	Solano (pen)	45,067
37	May	3	(h)	Birmingham City	W	1-0	Viana	52,146
38		11	(a)	West Bromwich Alb	D	2-2	Jenas, Viana	27,036

FINAL LEAGUE POSITION: 3rd in the F.A. Premiership

Appearances

Sub. Appearances

Goals

Appearances and goals grid (players as columns, matches 1–38 as rows):

#	Given SJJ	Hughes AW	Bernard O	Dyer KC	Bramble TM	Dabizas N	Solano NA	Jenas JA	Shearer A	Lua-Lua LT	Viana HMF	McClen J	Ameobi F	Elliott R	Speed GA	Griffin A	Bellamy CD	Robert L	O'Brien AJ	Caldwell S	Acuna DCW	Kerr B	Cort C	Woodgate JS	Ambrose D	Chopra M	#
1	1	2	3	4	5	6	7*	8	9	10†	11°	12	13	14													1
2	1	2	3†	4	5	6	7	8	9	10*	14		13			11°	12										2
3	1	2	3	4	5	6	7*	12	9	10†	11°		8					13	14								3
4	1	2	3	4	5		7		9		13		10†		8*	12	14	11	6°								4
5	1	2	3	4		6	7†	12	9		14		13		8		10°	11*	5								5
6	1		3	4		6	7°	12	9		14		13		8	2	10†	11*	5								6
7	1		3	4		6	7†	12	9	10*	14		13		8	2	11°		5								7
8	1		3	14	4	6	7†	12	9				13		8	2	10°	11*	5								8
9	1		3°	13	12	6	7	4	9		14				8	2*	10	11†	5								9
10	1		3	13	5		7†	4	9		12		10		8	2	11*	6									10
11	1	5	3	12			7†	4	9		13		10		8	2	11*	6									11
12	1		3	13	10	6	7†	4	9		11*		12		8	2			5								12
13	1		3	13	7		12	4	9		11*		10		8	2		5†	6								13
14	1		3	11*	7	6	12	4	9						8	2	10		5								14
15	1		3	4	7				9	13	12		8*		2	10	11	5	6†								15
16	1	6	3	4			7	8	9						2		10	11	5								16
17	1		3	7	4				9				8		2	10	11	5	6								17
18	1		3	4*			7†	12	9		13		8°		2	10	11	5	6	14							18
19	1		3	4			7*	12	9		13		10†		8	2	11	5	6								19
20	1	2	3	4*	12		7°	14	9		13		8†		10	11	5	6									20
21	1	6	3	4					9	12	13		2		10	11	5	8†	7*								21
22	1	5	3	7	4			12	9†		2		10		11		6	8*		13							22
23	1	2	3	4		6	7*	8	9				10		11		5	12									23
24	1	2	3	4		6	7*	8	9				10		11		5	12									24
25	1		3	4	2	6	12	8	9				10		11		5						7*				25
26	1	2	3	4	5		7*	8	9†		13		12		10		11		6								26
27	1		3	4°	5	12			9	14	8		2*		10	11		6				13	7†				27
28	1	2	3	4†	14		7°		9		11*		12	8		13	10		5					6			28
29	1	2	3	7	5		4		9		12		13	8*		10	11†							6			29
30	1	2	3	13	5		7†	4	9		11°		12	8*	14	10								6			30
31	1		3	4	5		7†	12	9°	14	13		8		2	10	11*							6			31
32	1		3	4	5			8	9		13		12	10	11		2†					7*		6			32
33	1	2	3	4	5		7*	8	9	14	13°		12	10	11†									6			33
34	1	4	3	8			7†		9	11*	13		2	10	5	12								6			34
35	1	4	3†	8	13		7	9°	12	11	14		2	10	5									6*			35
36	1		3	14	4		7	8	9†	11*	13		2	10	5°	12								6			36
37	1	2	3	4			7†	8	9	11*			10	13	5		12							6			37
38	1		3	4*			7†	8	9	10°	11				2			5	6	12					13	14	38
App	38	35	24	33	13	13	29	23	35	5	11		8		23	22	27	25	26	12	2	4		10			
Sub		6	2	3	3	2	9	6		12	1	20	2	1	5	2	2	2	2	4	1		1	1			
Gls			1	2	2		7	6	17	2	2		5		2	1	7	5		1							

2003-2004

#	Month	Date		Opponent	Res	Score	Scorers	Att
1	Aug	17	(a)	Leeds United	D	2-2	Shearer 2 (1 pen)	36,766
2		23	(h)	Manchester United	L	1-2	Shearer	52,165
3		30	(h)	Birmingham City	L	0-1		52,006
4	Sep	13	(a)	Everton	D	2-2	Shearer 2 (2 pens)	40,228
5		20	(h)	Bolton Wanderers	D	0-0		52,014
6		26	(a)	Arsenal	L	2-3	Robert, Bernard	38,112
7	Oct	4	(h)	Southampton	W	1-0	Shearer	52,127
8		18	(a)	Middlesbrough	W	1-0	Ameobi	34,081
9		21	(a)	Fulham	W	3-2	Robert, Shearer 2 (1 pen)	16,506
10		25	(h)	Portsmouth	W	3-0	Speed, Shearer (pen), Ameobi	52,161
11	Nov	1	(h)	Aston Villa	D	1-1	Robert	51,975
12		9	(a)	Chelsea	L	0-5		41,332
13		22	(h)	Manchester City	W	3-0	Ameobi, Shearer 2	52,159
14		29	(a)	Wolves	D	1-1	Shearer	29,344
15	Dec	6	(h)	Liverpool	D	1-1	Shearer (pen)	52,151
16		13	(h)	Tottenham Hotspur	W	4-0	Robert 2, Shearer 2	52,139
17		20	(a)	Charlton Athletic	D	0-0		26,508
18		26	(a)	Leicester City	D	1-1	Ambrose	32,148
19		28	(h)	Blackburn Rovers	L	0-1		51,648
20	Jan	7	(h)	Leeds United	W	1-0	Shearer	52,130
21		11	(a)	Manchester United	D	0-0		67,622
22		19	(h)	Fulham	W	3-1	O'Brien, Speed, Robert	50,104
23		31	(a)	Birmingham City	D	1-1	Speed	29,513
24	Feb	7	(h)	Leicester City	W	3-1	Ameobi, Taggart (og), Jenas	52,125
25		11	(a)	Blackburn Rovers	D	1-1	Bellamy	23,459
26		21	(h)	Middlesbrough	W	2-1	Bellamy, Shearer (pen)	52,156
27		29	(a)	Portsmouth	D	1-1	Bellamy	20,140
28	Mar	14	(a)	Tottenham Hotspur	L	0-1		36,083
29		20	(h)	Charlton Athletic	W	3-1	Shearer 2, Jenas	51,847
30		28	(a)	Bolton Wanderers	L	0-1		27,360
31	Apr	3	(h)	Everton	W	4-2	Bellamy, Dyer, Shearer 2	42,155
32		11	(h)	Arsenal	D	0-0		52,141
33		18	(a)	Aston Villa	D	0-0		40,786
34		25	(h)	Chelsea	W	2-1	Ameobi, Shearer	52,016
35	May	1	(a)	Manchester City	L	0-1		47,226
36		9	(h)	Wolves	D	1-1	Bowyer	52,139
37		12	(a)	Southampton	D	3-3	Ameobi, Bowyer, Ambrose	31,815
38		15	(a)	Liverpool	D	1-1	Ameobi	44,172

FINAL LEAGUE POSITION: 5th in the F.A. Premiership

Appearances

Sub. Appearances

Goals

Given SJ	Hughes AW	Bernard O	Dyer KC	O'Brien AJ	Woodgate JS	Bowyer LD	Speed GA	Shearer A	Bellamy CD	Robert L	Jenas JA	Ameobi F	Solano NA	Griffin A	Bramble TM	Chopra M	Viana HMF	Ambrose D	Lua-Lua LT	Caldwell S	Bridges M	Taylor S	Brittain M	#
1	2	3*	4	5	6	7†	8	9	10	11°	12	13	14											1
1	3		4	5		7*	8	9		11°	12	10†		2	6	13	14							2
1			4	5		12	3	9		14	8	10†	7*	2	6	13	11°							3
1		3	4	5		7	8*	9	10	11	12			2	6									4
1		3	4		6		8†	9	10	11	13	12	7*	2	5									5
1	2	3	4	5		8†	13	9	10	11°	7*	12			6			14						6
1	2	3	4	5		11	8	9	10		7				6									7
1	2	3	4	5		11*	8	9		12	7	10			6									8
1	2	3		5		7	8	9		11*	4	10			6			12						9
1	2	3		5		7*	8	9		11°	4	10†			6		14	12	13					10
1	2	3				7	8	9		11	4	10			5					6				11
1	2	3		5		7	8			11†	4	9			6	10*			13	12				12
1	2	3	7*		6	12	8	9		11°	4	10†			5			14	13					13
1	2	3	7		6	11†	8	9			4	13	12		5				10*					14
1	2*	3	7		6		8	9		11	4	10	12		5									15
1	2	3	7	12	6*		8†	9		11°	4	10	13		5			14						16
1	6	3	7	5			8	9		11†	4	10*	2					13	12					17
1	2*	3		5			8	9		11	4		7		6	13		12	10†					18
1	2	3		5		8†		9		11	4		7°		6	10°	13	12	14					19
1	2	3	10		6		8	9		11†	4		7*		5		13	12						20
1	2	3	10	5	6		8	9		11	4		7*					12						21
1	2	3	10	5	6		8	9†		11°	4	13	7*				14	12						22
1	2	3	10	5	6		8	9	12	11†	4							13	7*					23
1	2	3	7*	5	6		8	9†	14		4	10†						11	12		13			24
1	2	3	7	5			8	9	10	11	4				6									25
1	2	3	4	5		12	8	9	10	11					6			7*						26
1	2	3	4*	5		7†	8	9	10	11°	12				6		14				13			27
1	2*	3		5	6	7†	8	9	10	11	4	12						13						28
1	2*	3		5	6	13	8	9		11	4	10			12			7†						29
1		3			6	7†	8	9	10	11°	4*	14			5		12	13		2				30
1	2	3	4		6	12	8	9	10	11†		13			5			7*						31
1	2	3		5	6	12	8	9	10	11†	4						13	7*						32
1	2	3	7	5	6	12	8	9	10†	11*	4°							14			13			33
1	2	3		5	6*		8	9		11		10†			12		4	7			13			34
1	2	3		5			8	9		11°		10†			6	12	4	7*			13	14		35
1	2	3				4	8	9		11†		10			5	12	13	7*		6				36
1	2	3	11†			4	8	9		13		10			5*			7		6	12			37
1	3		11	5		4	8	9	14	13		10°		2*	6			7†		12				38
38	34	35	25	27	18	17	37	37	13	31	26	18	8	5	27	1	5	10	2	3	1			
				1		7	1		3	4	5	8	4		2	5	11	14	5	2	6	1		
	1	1	1			2	3	22	4	6	2	7						2						

F.A. CUP COMPETITION

1974/75 SEASON
3rd Round (at Maine Road by F.A. order)
Jan 3 vs Manchester City (a) 2-0
Att: 37,625   Nulty, Burns

4th Round
Jan 25 vs Walsall (a) 0-1
Att: 19,998

1975/76 SEASON
3rd Round
Jan 3 vs Queen's Park Rangers (a) 0-0
Att: 20,102

Replay
Jan 7 vs Queen's Park Rangers (h) 2-1
Att: 37,225   Craig T (pen), Gowling

4th Round
Jan 24 vs Coventry City (a) 1-1
Att: 32,004   Gowling

Replay
Jan 28 vs Coventry City (h) 5-0
*Att: 44,676   Gowling, Macdonald 2, Cassidy,
Burns*

5th Round
Feb 14 vs Bolton Wanderers (a) 3-3
Att: 46,880   Gowling, Macdonald 2

Replay
Feb 18 vs Bolton Wanderers (h) 0-0
Att: 52,760

2nd Replay (at Elland Road)
Feb 23 vs Bolton Wanderers 2-1
Att: 43,448   Gowling, Burns

6th Round
Mar 6 vs Derby County (a) 2-4
Att: 38,362   Gowling 2

1976/77 SEASON
3rd Round
Jan 8 vs Sheffield United (a) 0-0
Att: 30,513

Replay
Jan 24 vs Sheffield United (h) 3-1
Att: 36,375   Craig T, Burns, McCaffery

4th Round
Jan 29 vs Manchester City (h) 1-3
Att: 45,300   Gowling

1977/78 SEASON
3rd Round
Jan 7 vs Peterborough United (a) 1-1
Att: 17,621   Hudson

Replay
Jan 11 vs Peterborough United (h) 2-0
Att: 26,837   Craig T (pen), Blackhall

4th Round
Jan 28 vs Wrexham (h) 2-2
Att: 29,344   Bird, Blackhall

Replay
Feb 6 vs Wrexham (a) 1-4
Att: 18,676   Burns

1978/79 SEASON
3rd Round
Jan 16 vs Torquay United (h) 3-1
Att: 21,366   Robinson, Withe, Nattrass (pen)

4th Round
Jan 27 vs Wolverhampton Wands. (h) 1-1
Att: 29,561   Withe

Replay
Feb 22 vs Wolverhampton Wands. (a) 0-1
Att: 19,588

1979/80 SEASON
3rd Round
Jan 5 vs Chester (h) 0-2
Att: 24,548

1980/81 SEASON
3rd Round
Jan 3 vs Sheffield Wednesday (h) 2-1
Att: 22,458   Waddle 2

4th Round
Jan 24 vs Luton Town (h) 2-1
Att: 29,211   Clarke, Martin

5th Round
Feb 14 vs Exeter City (h) 1-1
Att: 36,984   Shoulder

Replay
Feb 18 vs Exeter City (a) 0-4
Att: 17,668

1981/82 SEASON
3rd Round
Jan 4 vs Colchester United (h) 1-1
Att: 16,977   Varadi

Replay
Jan 18 vs Colchester United (a) 4-3
*Att: 7,505   Waddle, Varadi, Saunders,
Brownlie*

4th Round
Jan 23 vs Grimsby Town (h) 1-2
Att: 25,632   Moore (og)

1982/83 SEASON
3rd Round
Jan 8 vs Brighton & Hove Albion (a) 1-1
Att: 17,711   McDermott

Replay
Jan 12 vs Brighton & Hove Albion (h) 0-1
Att: 32,687

1983/84 SEASON
3rd Round
Jan 6 vs Liverpool (a) 0-4
Att: 33,566

1984/85 SEASON
3rd Round
Jan 6 vs Nottingham Forest (a) 1-1
Att: 23,582   Megson

Replay
Jan 9 vs Nottingham Forest (h) 1-3 (aet.)
Att: 25,166   Waddle

1985/86 SEASON
3rd Round
Jan 4 vs Brighton & Hove Albion (h) 0-2
Att: 24,643

1986/87 SEASON
3rd Round
Jan 21 vs Northampton (h) 2-1
Att: 23,177   Goddard, Thomas A

4th Round
Jan 31 vs Preston North End (h) 2-0
Att: 30,495   Roeder, Goddard

5th Round
Feb 21 vs Tottenham Hotspur (a) 0-1
Att: 38,033

1987/88 SEASON
3rd Round
Jan 9 vs Crystal Palace (h) 1-0
Att: 20,203   Gascoigne

4th Round
Jan 30 vs Swindon Town (h) 5-0
*Att: 27,548   Jackson D, Gascoigne 2 (1 pen),
O'Neill, Goddard*

5th Round
Feb 20 vs Wimbledon (h) 1-3
Att: 28,796   McDonald

1988/89 SEASON
3rd Round
Jan 7 vs Watford (h) 0-0
Att: 24,086

Replay
Jan 10 vs Watford (a) 2-2 (aet.)
Att: 16,431   Brock, Mirandinha (pen)

2nd Replay
Jan 16 vs Watford (h) 0-0 (aet.)
Att: 28,370

3rd Replay
Jan 18 vs Watford (a) 0-1 (aet.)
Att: 15,115

1989/90 SEASON
3rd Round
Jan 6 vs Hull City (a) 1-0
Att: 10,743   O'Brien

4th Round
Jan 27 vs Reading (a) 3-3
Att: 11,989   Quinn, McGhee 2

Replay
Jan 31 vs Reading (h) 4-1
Att: 26,233   McGhee 2, Quinn, Robinson

5th Round
Feb 18 vs Manchester United (h) 2-3
Att: 31,748   McGhee (pen), Scott

1990/91 SEASON
3rd Round
Jan 5 vs Derby County (h) 2-0
Att: 19,748   Quinn, Stimson

4th Round
Feb 13 vs Nottingham Forest (h) 2-2
Att: 29,231   Quinn, McGhee

Replay
Feb 18 vs Nottingham Forest (a) 0-3
Att: 28,962

1991/92 SEASON
3rd Round
Jan 4 vs Bournemouth (a) 0-0
Att: 10,651

Replay
Jan 22 vs Bournemouth (h) 2-2 (aet.)
Att: 25,954   Hunt 2
Bournemouth won 4-3 on penalties

1992/93 SEASON
3rd Round
Jan 2 vs Port Vale (h) 4-0
Att: 29,873   Peacock 2, Lee, Sheedy

4th Round
Jan 23 vs Rotherham United (a) 1-1
Att: 13,405   Lee

Replay
Feb 3 vs Rotherham United (h) 2-0
Att: 29,005   Kelly, Clark

5th Round
Feb 13 vs Blackburn Rovers (a) 0-1
Att: 19,972

1993/94 SEASON
3rd Round
Jan 8 vs Coventry City (h) 2-0
Att: 35,444   Cole, Beardsley

4th Round
Jan 29 vs Luton Town (h) 1-1
Att: 32,216   Beardsley (pen)

Replay
Feb 9 vs Luton Town (a) 0-2
Att: 12,503

1994/95 SEASON
3rd Round
Jan 8 vs Blackburn Rovers (h) 1-1
Att: 31,721   Lee

Replay
Jan 18 vs Blackburn Rovers (a) 2-1
Att: 22,658   Hottiger, Clark

4th Round
Jan 28 vs Swansea City (h) 3-0
Att: 34,372   Kitson 3

5th Round
Feb 19 vs Manchester City (h) 3-1
Att: 33,219 Gillespie 2, Beresford

6th Round
Mar 12 vs Everton (a) 0-1
Att: 35,203

1995/96 SEASON
3rd Round
Jan 7 vs Chelsea (a) 1-1
Att: 25,151 Ferdinand

Replay
Jan 17 vs Chelsea (h) 2-2 (aet.)
Att: 36,535 Albert, Beardsley (pen)
Chelsea won 4-2 on penalties

1996/97 SEASON
3rd Round
Jan 5 vs Charlton Athletic (a) 1-1
Att: 15,000 Lee

Replay
Jan 15 vs Charlton Athletic (h) 2-1
Att: 36,398 Clark, Shearer

4th Round
Jan 26 vs Nottingham Forest (h) 1-2
Att: 36,434 Ferdinand

1997/98 SEASON
3rd Round
Jan 4 vs Everton (a) 1-0
Att: 20,885 Rush

4th Round
Jan 25 vs Stevenage Borough (a) 1-1
Att: 8,040 Shearer

Replay
Feb 4 vs Stevenage Borough (h) 2-1
Att: 36,705 Shearer 2

5th Round
Feb 14 vs Tranmere Rovers (h) 1-0
Att: 36,675 Shearer

6th Round
Mar 8 vs Barnsley (h) 3-1
Att: 36,695 Ketsbaia, Speed, Batty

Semi-Final (at Old Trafford)
Apr 5 vs Sheffield United 1-0
Att: 53,452 Shearer

FINAL (at Wembley)
May 16 vs Arsenal 0-2
Att: 79,183

1998/99 SEASON
3rd Round
Jan 2 vs Crystal Palace (h) 2-1
Att: 36,536 Speed, Shearer

4th Round
Jan 23 vs Bradford City (h) 3-0
Att: 36,698 Hamann, Shearer, Ketsbaia

5th Round
Feb 14 vs Blackburn Rovers (h) 0-0
Att: 36,295

Replay
Feb 24 vs Blackburn Rovers (a) 1-0
Att: 27,483 Saha

6th Round
Mar 7 vs Everton (h) 4-1
Att: 36,504 Ketsbaia 2, Georgiadis, Shearer

Semi-Final (at Old Trafford)
Apr 11 vs Tottenham Hotspur (h) 2-0
Att: 53,609 Shearer 2 (1 pen)

FINAL (at Wembley)
May 22 vs Manchester United 0-2
Att: 79,101

1999/2000 SEASON
3rd Round
Dec 12 vs Tottenham Hotspur (a) 1-1
Att: 33,116 Speed

Replay
Dec 22 vs Tottenham Hotspur (h) 6-1
Att: 35,415 Speed, Dabizas, Ferguson, Dyer,
Shearer 2 (1 pen)

4th Round
Jan 8 vs Sheffield United (h) 4-1
Att: 36,220 Shearer, Dabizas, Ferguson,
Gallacher

5th Round
Jan 31 vs Blackburn Rovers (a) 2-1
Att: 29,946 Shearer 2

6th Round
Feb 20 vs Tranmere Rovers (a) 3-2
Att: 15,776 Speed, Domi, Ferguson

Semi-Final (at Wembley)
Apr 9 vs Chelsea 1-2
Att: 73,876 Lee

2000/2001 SEASON
3rd Round
Jan 7 vs Aston Villa (h) 1-1
Att: 37,862 Solano

Replay
Jan 17 vs Aston Villa (a) 0-1
Att: 25,387

2001/2002 SEASON
3rd Round
Jan 5 vs Crystal Palace (h) 2-0
Att: 38,089 Shearer, Acuna

4th Round
Jan 27 vs Peterborough United (a) 4-2
Att: 13,841 O'Brien, McClen, Shearer,
Hughes

5th Round
Feb 17 vs Manchester City (h) 1-0
Att: 51,020 Solano

6th Round
Mar 9 vs Arsenal (h) 1-1
Att: 51,027 Robert

Replay
Mar 23 vs Arsenal (a) 0-3
Att: 38,073

2002/2003 SEASON
3rd Round
Jan 5 vs Wolverhampton Wanderers (a) 2-3
Att: 27,316 Jenas, Shearer (pen)

2003/2004 SEASON
3rd Round
Jan 3 vs Southampton (a) 3-0
Att: 28,456 Dyer 2, Robert

4th Round
Jan 24 vs Liverpool (a) 1-2
Att: 41,365 Robert

LEAGUE CUP COMPETITION

1974/75 SEASON
2nd Round
Sep 10 vs Nottingham Forest (a) 1-1
Att: 14,183 Macdonald

Replay
Sep 25 vs Nottingham Forest (h) 3-0
Att: 26,228 Macdonald, Burns, Keeley

3rd Round
Oct 8 vs Queen's Park Rangers (a) 4-0
Att: 15,815 Tudor, Macdonald 3

4th Round
Nov 13 vs Fulham (h) 3-0
Att: 23,774 Cannell, Macdonald, Cassidy

5th Round
Dec 4 vs Chester (h) 0-0
Att: 31,656

Replay
Dec 18 vs Chester (a) 0-1
Att: 19,000

1975/76 SEASON
2nd Round (Scheduled at Southport but
played at Newcastle by agreement)
Sep 10 vs Southport (h) 6-0
Att: 23,352 Gowling 4, Cannell 2

3rd Round
Oct 7 vs Bristol Rovers (a) 1-1
Att: 17,141 Gowling

Replay
Oct 15 vs Bristol Rovers (h) 2-0
Att: 26,294 Craig T (pen), Nattrass

4th Round
Nov 11 vs Queen's Park Rangers (a) 3-1
Att: 21,162 Macdonald, Burns, Nulty

5th Round
Dec 3 vs Notts County (h) 1-0
Att: 31,114 McManus (og)

Semi-Final (1st leg)
Jan 14 vs Tottenham Hotspur (h) 0-1
Att: 40,215

Semi-Final (2nd leg)
Jan 21 vs Tott. Hotspur (h) 3-1 (agg. 3-2)
Att: 49,902 Gowling, Keeley, Nulty

FINAL (at Wembley)
Feb 28 vs Manchester City 1-2
Att: 100,000 Gowling

1976/77 SEASON
2nd Round
Sep 1 vs Gillingham (a) 2-1
Att: 11,203 Cassidy, Cannell

3rd Round
Sep 22 vs Stoke City (h) 3-0
Att: 27,143 Craig T (pen), Burns, Nattrass

4th Round
Oct 27 vs Manchester United (h) 2-7
Att: 45,300 Burns, Nattrass

1977/78 SEASON
2nd Round
Aug 31 vs Millwall (h) 0-1
Att: 21,861

1978/79 SEASON
2nd Round
Aug 29 vs Watford (a) 1-2
Att: 15,346 Pearson

1979/80 SEASON
2nd Round (1st leg)
Aug 29 vs Sunderland (a) 2-2
Att: 27,746 Davies, Cartwright

2nd Round (2nd leg)
Sep 5 vs Sunderland (h) 2-2 (aet) (agg. 4-4)
Att: 30,533 Shoulder, Boam
Sunderland won 7-6 on penalties

1980/81 SEASON
2nd Round (1st leg)
Aug 27 vs Bury (h) 3-2
Att: 9,073 Rafferty 2, Shoulder

2nd Round (2nd leg)
Sep 2 vs Bury (a) 0-1 (aggregate 3-3)
Att: 4,348 Bury won on Away Goals

1981/82 SEASON
2nd Round (1st leg)
Oct 7 vs Fulham (h) 1-2
Att: 20,247 Barton

2nd Round (2nd leg)
Oct 28 vs Fulham (a) 0-2 (aggregate 1-4)
Att: 7,210

1982/83 SEASON
2nd Round (1st leg)
Oct 6 vs Leeds United (a) 1-0
Att: 24,012 Varadi

2nd Round (2nd leg)
Oct 27 vs Leeds United (h) 1-4 (agg. 2-4)
Att: 24,984   Clarke

1983/84 SEASON
2nd Round (1st leg)
Oct 5 vs Oxford United (h) 1-1
Att: 21,167   McDermott

2nd Round (2nd leg)
Oct 26 vs Oxford United (a) 1-2 (agg. 2-3)
Att: 13,040   Keegan

1984/85 SEASON
2nd Round (1st leg)
Sep 26 vs Bradford City (h) 3-1
Att: 18,121   McDonald, Ferris, Watson

2nd Round (2nd leg)
Oct 10 vs Bradford City (a) 1-0 (agg. 4-1)
Att: 10,210   Waddle

3rd Round
Oct 30 vs Ipswich Town (a) 1-1
Att: 15,084   McDonald

Replay
Nov 7 vs Ipswich Town (h) 1-2
Att: 22,982   Waddle

1985/86 SEASON
2nd Round (1st leg)
Sep 25 vs Barnsley (h) 0-0
Att: 18,544

2nd Round (2nd leg)
Oct 7 vs Barnsley (a) 1-1 (aet.)
Att: 10,084   Cunningham
Newcastle won on Away Goals

3rd Round
Oct 30 vs Oxford United (a) 1-3
Att: 8,096   Cunningham

1986/87 SEASON
2nd Round (1st leg)
Sep 23 vs Bradford City (a) 0-2
Att: 6,384

2nd Round (2nd leg)
Oct 8 vs Bradford City (h) 1-0 (agg. 1-2)
Att: 15,803   Roeder

1987/88 SEASON
2nd Round (1st leg)
Sep 23 vs Blackpool (a) 0-1
Att: 7,691

2nd Round (2nd leg)
Oct 7 vs Blackpool (h) 4-1 (aggregate 4-2)
Att: 20,808   Goddard, Mirandinha,
Jackson D, Gascoigne

3rd Round
Oct 28 vs Wimbledon (a) 1-2
Att: 6,443   McDonald (pen)

1988/89 SEASON
2nd Round (1st leg)
Sep 27 vs Sheffield United (a) 0-3
Att: 17,900

2nd Round (2nd leg)
Oct 12 vs Sheffield United (h) 2-0 (agg. 2-3)
Att: 14,520   Hendrie, Mirandinha

1989/90 SEASON
2nd Round (1st leg)
Sep 19 vs Reading (a) 1-3
Att: 7,960   Gallacher

2nd Round (2nd leg)
Oct 4 vs Reading (h) 4-0 (aggregate 5-3)
Att: 15,220   Brazil (pen), Brock, Thorn,
McGhee

3rd Round
Oct 25 vs West Bromwich Albion (h) 0-1
Att: 22,639

1990/91 SEASON
2nd Round (1st leg)
Sep 25 vs Middlesbrough (a) 0-2
Att: 15,042

2nd Round (2nd leg)
Oct 10 vs Middlesbrough (h) 1-0 (agg. 1-2)
Att: 12,778   Anderson

1991/92 SEASON
2nd Round (1st leg)
Sep 24 vs Crewe Alexandra (a) 4-3
Att: 4,251   Hunt, Peacock 3

2nd Round (2nd leg)
Oct 9 vs Crewe Alexandra (h) 1-0 (agg. 5-3)
Att: 9,197   Howey

3rd Round
Oct 29 vs Peterborough United (a) 0-1
Att: 10,382

1992/93 SEASON
1st Round (1st leg)
Aug 19 vs Mansfield Town (h) 2-1
Att: 14,083   Peacock 2

1st Round (2nd leg)
Aug 25 vs Mansfield Town (a) 0-0 (agg. 2-1)
Att: 6,725

2nd Round (1st leg)
Sep 23 vs Middlesbrough (h) 0-0
Att: 25,814

2nd Round (2nd leg)
Oct 7 vs Middlesbrough (a) 3-1 (agg. 3-1)
Att: 24,390   Kelly 2, O'Brien

3rd Round
Oct 28 vs Chelsea (a) 1-2
Att: 30,193   Lee

1993/94 SEASON
2nd Round (1st leg)
Sep 22 vs Notts County (h) 4-1
Att: 25,887   Cole 3, Bracewell

2nd Round (2nd leg)
Oct 5 vs Notts County (a) 7-1 (agg. 11-2)
Att: 6,068   Allen 2 (1 pen), Beardsley, Cole 3,
Lee

3rd Round
Oct 27 vs Wimbledon (a) 1-2
Att: 11,531   Sellars

1994/95 SEASON
2nd Round (1st leg)
Sep 21 vs Barnsley (h) 2-1
Att: 27,208   Cole, Fox

2nd Round (2nd leg)
Oct 5 vs Barnsley (a) 1-0 (aggregate 3-1)
Att: 10,992   Cole

3rd Round
Oct 26 vs Manchester United (h) 2-0
Att: 34,178   Albert, Kitson

4th Round
Nov 30 vs Manchester City (a) 1-1
Att: 25,162   Jeffrey

Replay
Dec 21 vs Manchester City (h) 0-2
Att: 30,156

1995/96 SEASON
2nd Round (1st leg)
Sep 19 vs Bristol City (a) 5-0
Att: 15,592   Peacock, Sellars, Ferdinand,
Gillespie, Lee

2nd Round (2nd leg)
Oct 4 vs Bristol City (h) 3-1 (agg. 8-1)
Att: 36,357   Barton, Albert, Ferdinand

3rd Round
Oct 25 vs Stoke City (a) 4-0
Att: 23,000   Beardsley 2, Ferdinand, Peacock

4th Round
Nov 29 vs Liverpool (a) 1-0
Att: 40,077   Watson

5th Round
Jan 10 vs Arsenal (a) 0-2
Att: 37,857

1996/97 SEASON
3rd Round
Oct 23 vs Oldham Athletic (h) 1-0
Att: 36,314   Beardsley (pen)

4th Round
Nov 27 vs Middlesbrough (a) 1-3
Att: 29,831   Shearer

1997/98 SEASON
3rd Round
Oct 15 vs Hull City (h) 2-0
Att: 35,856   Hamilton, Rush

4th Round
Nov 18 vs Derby County (a) 1-0
Att: 27,364   Tomasson

5th Round
Jan 7 vs Liverpool (h) 0-2
Att: 33,207

1998/99 SEASON
3rd Round
Oct 27 vs Tranmere Rovers (a) 1-0
Att: 12,017   Dalglish

4th Round
Nov 11 vs Blackburn Rovers (h) 1-1 (aet)
Att: 34,702   Shearer
Blackburn Rovers won 4-2 on penalties

1999/2000 SEASON
3rd Round
Oct 12 vs Birmingham City (a) 0-2
Att: 19,795

2000/2001 SEASON
2nd Round (1st leg)
Sep 20 vs Leyton Orient (h) 2-0
Att: 37,284   Cort, Speed

2nd Round (2nd leg)
Sep 26 vs Leyton Orient (a) 1-1 (agg. 3-1)
Att: 9,522   Gallacher

3rd Round
Nov 1 vs Bradford City (h) 4-3
Att: 41,847   Shearer 2, Cordone, Caldwell

4th Round
Nov 29 vs Birmingham City (a) 1-2
Att: 18,520   Dyer

2001/2002 SEASON
2nd Round
Sep 12 vs Brentford (h) 4-1
Att: 25,633   Ameobi, Bellamy 3

3rd Round
Oct 9 vs Barnsley (a) 1-0
Att: 14,493   Bellamy

4th Round
Nov 27 vs Ipswich Town (h) 4-1
Att: 32,576   Robert, Ameobi, Shearer 2

5th Round
Dec 12 vs Chelsea (a) 0-1
Att: 27,613

2002/2003 SEASON
3rd Round
Nov 6 vs Everton (h) 3-3 (aet)
Att: 34,584   Dyer 2, Pistone (og)
Everton won 3-2 on penalties

2003/2004 SEASON
3rd Round
Oct 29 vs West Brom. Albion (h) 1-2 (aet)
Att: 46,932   Robert

UEFA CUP COMPETITION

1977/78 SEASON
1st Round (1st leg)
Sep 14 vs Bohemians (a) 0-0
Att: 25,000

1st Round (2nd leg)
Sep 28 vs Bohemians (h) 4-0 (agg. 4-0)
Att: 19,046 Craig T 2, Gowling 2

2nd Round (1st leg)
Oct 19 vs Bastia (a) 1-2
Att: 8,500 Cannell

2nd Round (2nd leg)
Nov 2 vs Bastia (h) 1-3 (aggregate 2-5)
Att: 34,560 Gowling

1994/95 SEASON
1st Round (1st leg)
Sep 13 vs Antwerp (a) 5-0
Att: 19,700 Lee 3, Sellars, Watson

1st Round (2nd leg)
Sep 27 vs Antwerp (h) 5-2 (aggregate 10-2)
Att: 29,737 Lee, Cole 3, Beardsley (pen)

2nd Round (1st leg)
Oct 18 vs Athletic Bilbao (h) 3-2
Att: 32,140 Fox, Beardsley (pen), Cole

2nd Round (2nd leg)
Nov 1 vs Athletic Bilbao (a) 0-1 (agg. 3-3)
Att: 47,000
Athletic Bilbao won on Away Goals

1996/97 SEASON
1st Round (1st leg)
Sep 10 vs Halmstad (h) 4-0
Att: 28,124 Ferdinand, Asprilla, Albert, Beardsley

1st Round (2nd leg)
Sep 24 vs Halmstad (a) 1-2 (aggregate 5-2)
Att: 7,847 Ferdinand

2nd Round (1st leg)
Oct 15 vs Ferencvaros (a) 2-3
Att: 18,000 Ferdinand, Shearer

2nd Round (2nd leg)
Oct 29 vs Ferencvaros (h) 4-0 (agg. 6-3)
Att: 35,740 Asprilla 2, Ginola, Ferdinand

Quarter-Final (1st leg)
Mar 4 vs Monaco (h) 0-1
Att: 36,215

Quarter-Final (2nd leg)
Mar 18 vs Monaco (a) 0-3 (aggregate 0-4)
Att: 18,500

1999/2000 SEASON
1st Round (1st leg)
Sep 16 vs CSKA Sofia (a) 2-0
Att: 20,260 Solano, Ketsbaia

1st Round (2nd leg)
Sep 30 vs CSKA Sofia (h) 2-2 (agg. 4-2)
Att: 36,228 Shearer, Robinson

2nd Round (1st leg)
Oct 21 vs Zurich (a) 2-1
Att: 9,600 Maric, Shearer

2nd Round (2nd leg)
Nov 4 vs Zurich (h) 3-1 (aggregate 5-2)
Att: 34,502 Maric, Ferguson, Speed

3rd Round (1st leg)
Nov 25 vs Roma (a) 0-1
Att: 45,655

3rd Round (2nd leg)
Dec 9 vs Roma (h) 0-0 (aggregate 0-1)
Att: 35,739

2003/2004 SEASON
1st Round (1st leg)
Sep 24 vs NAC Breda (h) 5-0
Att: 36,007 Bellamy 2, Bramble, Shearer, Ambrose

1st Round (2nd leg)
Oct 15 vs NAC Breda (h) 1-0 (agg. 6-0)
Att: 16,400 Robert

2nd Round (1st leg)
Nov 6 vs FC Basel (a) 3-2
Att: 30,000 Robert, Bramble, Ameobi

2nd Round (2nd leg)
Nov 27 vs FC Basel (h) 1-0
Att: 40,295 Smiljanic (og)

3rd Round (1st leg)
Feb 26 vs Våleranga (a) 1-1
Att: 17,039 Bellamy

3rd Round (2nd leg)
Mar 4 vs Våleranga (h) 3-1 (aggregate 4-2)
Att: 38,531 Shearer, Ameobi 2

4th Round (1st leg)
Mar 11 vs Real Mallorca (h) 4-1
Att: 38,012 Bellamy, Shearer, Robert, Bramble

4th Round (2nd leg)
Mar 25 vs Real Mallorca (a) 3-0 (agg. 7-1)
Att: 11,500 Shearer 2, Bellamy

Quarter-Final (1st leg)
Apr 8 vs PSV Eindhoven (a) 1-1
Att: 35,000 Jenas

Quarter-Final (2nd leg)
Apr 14 vs PSV Eindhoven (h) 2-1 (agg. 3-2)
Att: 50,083 Shearer 2

Semi-Final (1st leg)
Apr 22 vs Marseille (h) 0-0
Att: 52,004

Semi-Final (2nd leg)
May 6 vs Marseille (a) 0-2 (aggregate 0-2)
Att: 57,500

EUROPEAN CHAMPIONS CUP

1997/98 SEASON
2nd Qualifying Round (1st leg)
Aug 13 vs Croatia Zagreb (h) 2-1
Att: 34,465 Beresford 2

2nd Qualifying Round (2nd leg)
Aug 27 vs Croatia Zagreb (a) 2-2 (agg. 4-3)
Att: 34,000 Asprilla (pen), Ketsbaia

Group C, Game 1
Sep 17 vs Barcelona (h) 3-2
Att: 35,274 Asprilla 3 (1 pen)

Group C, Game 2
Oct 1 vs Dynamo Kiev (a) 2-2
Att: 100,000 Beresford 2

Group C, Game 3
Oct 22 vs PSV Eindhoven (a) 0-1
Att: 29,200

Group C, Game 4
Nov 5 vs PSV Eindhoven (h) 0-2
Att: 35,214

Group C, Game 5
Nov 26 vs Barcelona (a) 0-1
Att: 25,000

Group C, Game 6
Dec 10 vs Dynamo Kiev (h) 2-0
Att: 33,694 Barnes, Pearce

2002/2003 SEASON
3rd Qualifying Round (1st leg)
Aug 14 vs Zeljeznicar (a) 1-0
Att: 36,000 Dyer

3rd Qualifying Round (2nd leg)
Aug 28 vs Zeljeznicar (h) 4-0 (agg. 5-0)
Att: 34,067 Dyer, Lua-Lua, Viana, Shearer

Group E, Game 1
Sep 18 vs Dynamo Kiev (a) 0-2
Att: 42,500

Group E, Game 2
Sep 24 vs Feyenoord (h) 0-1
Att: 40,540

Group E, Game 3
Oct 1 vs Juventus (a) 0-2
Att: 41,424

Group E, Game 4
Oct 23 vs Juventus (h) 1-0
Att: 48,370 Buffon (og)

Group E, Game 5
Oct 29 vs Dynamo Kiev (h) 2-1
Att: 40,185 Speed, Shearer (pen)

Group E, Game 6
Nov 13 vs Feyenoord (a) 3-2
Att: 45,000 Bellamy 2, Viana

2nd Stage, Group A, Game 1
Nov 27 vs Internazionale (h) 1-4
Att: 50,108 Solano

2nd Stage, Group A, Game 2
Dec 11 vs Barcelona (a) 1-3
Att: 45,100 Ameobi

2nd Stage, Group A, Game 3
Feb 18 vs Leverkusen (a) 3-1
Att: 22,500 Ameobi 2, Lua-Lua

2nd Stage, Group A, Game 4
Feb 26 vs Leverkusen (h) 3-1
Att: 40,508 Shearer 3 (1 pen)

2nd Stage, Group A, Game 5
Mar 11 vs Internazionale (a) 2-2
Att: 53,459 Shearer 2

2nd Stage, Group A, Game 6
Mar 19 vs Barcelona (h) 0-2
Att: 51,883

2003/2004 SEASON
3rd Qualifying Round (1st leg)
Aug 13 vs Partizan Belgrade (a) 1-0
Att: 32,500 Solano

3rd Qualifying Round (2nd leg)
Aug 27 vs Partizan Belgrade (h) 0-1 (aet)
Att: 37,293
Partizan Belgrade won 4-3 on penalties

EUROPEAN CUP-WINNERS' CUP

1998/99 SEASON
1st Round (1st leg)
Sep 17 vs Partizan Belgrade (h) 2-1
Att: 26,599 Shearer, Dabizas

1st Round (2nd leg)
Oct 1 vs Partizan Belgrade (a) 0-1 (agg. 2-2)
Att: 26,000
Partizan won on the Away Goals rule

Supporters' Guides & Other Titles

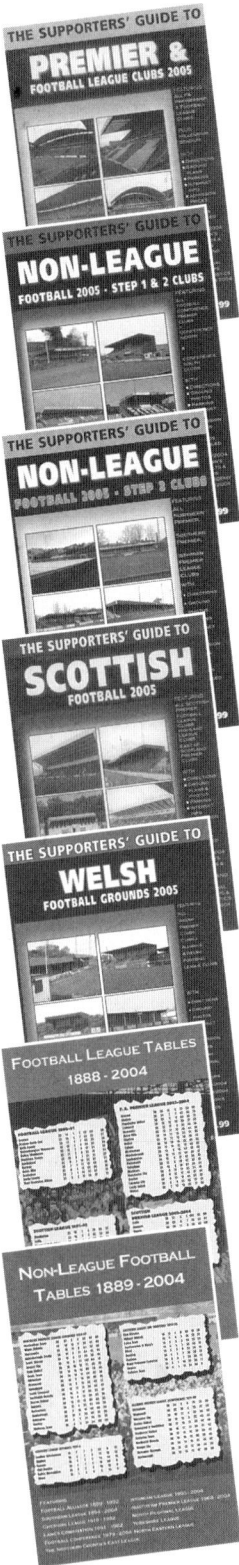

This top-selling series has been published annually since 1982 and contains 2003/2004 Season's results and tables, Directions, Photographs, Phone numbers, Parking information, Admission details, Disabled information and much more.

THE SUPPORTERS' GUIDE TO PREMIER & FOOTBALL LEAGUE CLUBS 2005

The 21st edition featuring all Premiership and Football League clubs. *Price £6.99*

THE SUPPORTERS' GUIDE TO NON-LEAGUE FOOTBALL 2005 – STEP 1 & STEP 2 CLUBS

Following the reorganisation of Non-League Football this 13th edition covers all 66 Step 1 & Step 2 clubs – effectively the Football Conference and it's feeder Leagues. *Price £6.99*

THE SUPPORTERS' GUIDE TO NON-LEAGUE FOOTBALL 2005 – STEP 3 CLUBS

Following the reorganisation of Non-League Football the 1st edition of this book features all 66 clubs which feed into the Football Conference. *Price £6.99*

THE SUPPORTERS' GUIDE TO SCOTTISH FOOTBALL 2005

The 13th edition featuring all Scottish Premier League, Scottish League and Highland League clubs. *Price £6.99*

THE SUPPORTERS' GUIDE TO WELSH FOOTBALL GROUNDS 2005

The 9th edition featuring all League of Wales, Cymru Alliance & Welsh Football League Clubs + results, tables & much more. *Price £6.99*

FOOTBALL LEAGUE TABLES 1888-2004

The 7th edition contains every Football League, Premier League, Scottish League and Scottish Premier League Final Table from 1888-2004 together with Cup Final Information. *Price £9.99*

NON-LEAGUE FOOTBALL TABLES 1889-2004

The 3rd edition contains final tables for the Conference, it's 3 feeder Leagues and 4 Northern Leagues in England (which were not included in previous editions). *Price £9.95*

These books are available UK & Surface post free from –

Soccer Books Limited (Dept. SBL)
72 St. Peter's Avenue
Cleethorpes
N.E. Lincolnshire
DN35 8HU